New D

Edited by **Sally Welch** May–August 2018

The Bible Reading Fellowship
15 The Chambers, Vineyard
Abingdon OX14 3FE
brf.org.uk

The Bible Reading Fellowship (BRF) is a Registered Charity (233280)

ISBN 978 0 85746 598 6
All rights reserved

This edition © The Bible Reading Fellowship 2018
Cover image and illustration on page 143 © Thinkstock

Distributed in Australia by:
MediaCom Education Inc, PO Box 610, Unley, SA 5061
Tel: 1 800 811 311 | admin@mediacom.org.au

Distributed in New Zealand by:
Scripture Union Wholesale, PO Box 760, Wellington
Tel: 04 385 0421 | suwholesale@clear.net.nz

Acknowledgements
The New Revised Standard Version of the Bible, Anglicised Edition, copyright © 1989,
1995 by the Division of Christian Education of the National Council of the Churches of
Christ in the USA. Used by permission. All rights reserved.

The Holy Bible, New International Version, Anglicised edition, copyright © 1979,
1984, 2011 by Biblica. Used by permission of Hodder & Stoughton Publishers, an
Hachette UK company. All rights reserved. 'NIV' is a registered trademark of Biblica.
UK trademark number 1448790.

The Revised Standard Version of the Bible, copyright © 1946, 1952, 1971 by the
Division of Christian Education of the National Council of the Churches of Christ in the
United States of America. Used by permission. All rights reserved.

Scripture quotations marked (GNT) are from the Good News Translation in Today's
English Version – Second Edition Copyright © 1992 by American Bible Society. Used
by permission.

Extracts from the Authorised Version of the Bible (The King James Bible), the rights in
which are vested in the Crown, are reproduced by permission of the Crown's Patentee,
Cambridge University Press.

Scripture taken from the New King James Version®. Copyright © 1982 by Thomas
Nelson. Used by permission. All rights reserved.

The Revised Common Lectionary is copyright © The Consultation on Common Texts,
1992 and is reproduced with permission. *The Christian Year: Calendar, Lectionary and
Collects*, which includes the *Common Worship* lectionary (the Church of England's
adaptations of the *Revised Common Lectionary*, published as the Principal Service
lectionary) is copyright © The Central Board of Finance of the Church of England,
1995, 1997, and material from it is reproduced with permission.

Printed by Gutenberg Press, Tarxien, Malta

Suggestions for using *New Daylight*

Find a regular time and place, if possible, where you can read and pray undisturbed. Before you begin, take time to be still and perhaps use the BRF Prayer on page 6. Then read the Bible passage slowly (try reading it aloud if you find it over-familiar), followed by the comment. You can also use *New Daylight* for group study and discussion, if you prefer.

The prayer or point for reflection can be a starting point for your own meditation and prayer. Many people like to keep a journal to record their thoughts about a Bible passage and items for prayer. In *New Daylight* we also note the Sundays and some special festivals from the church calendar, to keep in step with the Christian year.

New Daylight and the Bible

New Daylight contributors use a range of Bible versions, and you will find a list of the versions used opposite. You are welcome to use your own preferred version alongside the passage printed in the notes. This can be particularly helpful if the Bible text has been abridged.

New Daylight affirms that the whole of the Bible is God's revelation to us, and we should read, reflect on and learn from every part of both Old and New Testaments. Usually the printed comment presents a straightforward 'thought for the day', but sometimes it may also raise questions rather than simply providing answers, as we wrestle with some of the more difficult passages of Scripture.

New Daylight is also available in a deluxe edition (larger format). Visit your local Christian bookshop or contact the BRF office, who can also give details about a cassette version for the visually impaired. For a Braille edition, contact St John's Guild, Sovereign House, 12–14 Warwick Street, Coventry CV5 6ET.

Comment on *New Daylight*

To send feedback, please email **enquiries@brf.org.uk**, phone **+44 (0)1865 319700** or write to the address shown opposite.

Writers in this issue

Paul Gravelle is an Anglican priest in Auckland, New Zealand. He is a poet, writer and retreat leader and has ministered in military, urban and rural settings, supporting himself as an industrial journalist.

Tony Horsfall is a retreat leader and author based in Yorkshire who describes himself now as being 'semi-retired'. He is actively involved in his local church and tries to keep active by playing walking football and spending time with his grandchildren.

Lakshmi Jeffreys is the rector (vicar) of a parish just outside Northampton. She combines this with being a wife, mother, friend, dog-walker and school governor and fulfilling various other roles, within and beyond the wider church. Her booklet on singleness was published shortly after she met the man she eventually married.

Andy John is the Bishop of Bangor and has served there for nine years. Andy is a Kiwi (his mother's side) and Welsh cross (his father's side) and has spent all his ministry in the Church in Wales. Apart from being a bishop he occasionally attempts marathons (Snowdonia being a favourite) and enjoys time with his now grown-up children.

Bob Mayo is a writer, vicar and marathon-runner. He is an associate member of staff at St Mellitus London and St Michael's Cardiff. He lives in Shepherd's Bush in London and is chaplain to Queens Park Rangers. His publications include *Making Sense of Generation Y* (2006) and *The Faith of Generation Y* (2010). He is at his most comfortable walking with his wife and their two beloved dachshunds.

Michael Mitton works freelance in the areas of spirituality and mission. He is also the part-time Fresh Expressions Officer for Derby Diocese and the NSM Priest in Charge of St Paul's Derby. He is author of *Travellers of the Heart* (BRF 2013).

Barbara Mosse is a retired Anglican priest with experience in various chaplaincies and theological education. A freelance lecturer and retreat giver, her latest book for BRF is *Welcoming the Way of the Cross* (BRF, 2013).

Margaret Silf is an ecumenical Christian committed to working across and beyond traditional divisions. She is the author of a number of books for 21st-century spiritual pilgrims and a retreat facilitator. She is a mother and grandmother and lives in North Staffordshire.

Sally Welch writes...

By the time you read this, I will have spent another post-Easter break on a pilgrimage, that is a spiritual journey to a sacred place. I will have explored new surroundings in the intimate, close-up way which is only afforded by a journey on foot, allowing time for the landscape to soak into the soul, providing much material for reflection and appreciation. I will have been challenged by long days on the road, carrying a heavy pack, and delighted by the people and places I have encountered. These long, leisured journeys, sometimes made alone, sometimes in the company of others, give me the space I need to recharge and refresh, combining as they do physical challenge with spiritual revelation. In the light of this, it has been a joy to read Margaret Silf's reflections on mountains and roof-tops as she looks at the spiritual implications of high places and extreme locations. She shares with us the excitement and challenge of attaining such altitudes, as well as the pleasures and demands of a return to lower ground and everyday life. And in the midst of this everyday life I hope you will find a great resource in Tony Horsfall's helpful exploration of the themes of encouragement and challenge, which run in partnership throughout the Bible. Encouragement for periods of doubt and difficulty are balanced by the challenge set before us of continuing to grow in faith during both hard and easy times.

You will find both encouragement and challenge elsewhere in this edition, as I help us to see how the freedom we find in faith in Christ is both a marvellous gift and a great responsibility, while Michael Mitton shows us how we can take encouragement from those first disciples: 'for we too are ordinary mortals trying to follow Jesus along the perplexing pathways of this world'.

As we make our way together through this part of the year, with its long days and (we hope) warm temperatures, I pray you will find within these pages the nourishment you need to refresh and sustain you on your life's journey, as well as the gentle challenges that will help you grow deeper and stronger in faith and love.

Sally Ann Welch

The BRF Prayer

Almighty God,
you have taught us that your word is a lamp for our feet
and a light for our path. Help us, and all who prayerfully
read your word, to deepen our fellowship with you
and with each other through your love.
And in so doing may we come to know you more fully,
love you more truly, and follow more faithfully
in the steps of your son Jesus Christ, who lives and reigns
with you and the Holy Spirit, one God for evermore.
Amen

Studies on Psalms 81—93

When I was studying theology at college, we were told the psalms were 'the hymn book of the Bible', but a hymn book compiled in a complicated way. Most modern hymn books (for those churches and groups not used to electronically projected lyrics) are arranged either thematically according to, for example, the church year (Advent, Christmas, Epiphany and so on), alphabetically according to the first line, or both. While the 150 psalms in the Bible are organised into five books, scholars vary in their ideas as to the distinctive nature of any particular book.

There are different suggestions for themes in the psalms. For example, some divide the psalter into such categories as hymns, communal laments, individual laments, royal psalms, individual thanksgiving and communal thanksgiving. Walter Brueggemann, who has spent a lifetime studying the Book of Psalms, suggests: psalms of orientation, for seasons of well-being, joy, delight, coherence and order; psalms of disorientation, for seasons of hurt, alienation, suffering and death (including such emotions as self-pity and hatred); psalms of new orientation, for seasons of surprise, new gifts and joy breaking through despair. There are links between this scheme and the life of Jesus (birth, death, resurrection/kingship), and readers might want to research further.

Jesus was intimately familiar with the psalms through individual study and corporate worship. Many ancient hymns and modern worship songs use sections of psalms to praise God or cry out in despair. The following studies offer consecutive psalms as aids to prayer and worship, although within this there are also theological ideas. Perhaps the more we learn about God (theology) the more fully we can worship God. The headings are largely adapted from the *Word Biblical Commentary, Volume 20: Psalms 51–100* by Marvin Tate (Word, 1990) and can be used as an aid to worship.

In most cases only a few verses of any psalm are quoted. It is worth reading the whole psalm to gain a fuller understanding of what is being said or sung. Finally, invite the Holy Spirit to aid your worship. I often find through *New Daylight* that God addresses my particular circumstances on a specific day with the set reading. However, you might want to look at the heading and read the psalm out of order.

LAKSHMI JEFFREYS

God's appeal to his stubborn people

I am the Lord your God, who brought you up out of the land of Egypt. Open your mouth wide and I will fill it. But my people did not listen to my voice; Israel would not submit to me. So I gave them over to their stubborn hearts, to follow their own counsels. O that my people would listen to me, that Israel would walk in my ways! Then I would quickly subdue their enemies, and turn my hand against their foes.

The opening of this psalm seems to be a joyful invitation to take part in a celebration initiated by God when Joseph went to Egypt. There is then a reminder that God rescued his people when they cried out to him, before testing them at the waters of Meribah.

Today's passage shows the longing of God for his people. This is no distant, abstract power, aloof from creation. Yahweh (the name of God, written 'Lord') is affected by how his people behave. The God who has power to save is moved by the disobedience of those to whom he has shown extraordinary love. Had the people listened to the Lord, he would have overcome their enemies. Not only this, God would provide the very best for his people. Perhaps the greatest punishment he can mete out is to let them live with the consequences of their actions. They have chosen to ignore their saviour; God will allow them to experience the result of life without him.

A friend made unwise choices that resulted in his marriage ending. He was in tears as he recalled his marriage declarations, to love, comfort, honour and protect his bride and forsake all others to be faithful to her as long as they both lived. Other people had highlighted the possible consequences of his actions but he had ignored them. While there would eventually be forgiveness and a level of reconciliation, the man was aware too late of how he had taken his wife and her love for him for granted.

Through Jesus we can know forgiveness and healing when we forget God's love and provision. How might we not take this for granted?

LAKSHMI JEFFREYS

A plea for justice

God has taken his place in the divine council; in the midst of the gods he holds judgement: 'How long will you judge unjustly and show partiality to the wicked? Give justice to the weak and the orphan; maintain the right of the lowly and the destitute. Rescue the weak and the needy; deliver them from the hand of the wicked.' They have neither knowledge nor understanding, they walk around in darkness; all the foundations of the earth are shaken.

Today's psalm appears to challenge the notion of one true God, with its depiction of an assembly of gods. In the West we often forget the heavenly realms with authorities and powers. As we are reminded in Ephesians 6:12, 'our struggle is not against enemies of blood and flesh, but against the rulers, against the authorities, against the cosmic powers of this present darkness, against the spiritual forces of evil in the heavenly places.' The heavenly powers might influence people, but individuals and nations still have choices about how they act and, under the living God, can resist malign forces.

Here God has an overwhelming passion for justice for those who have no voice, no status, no wealth and no power. This is a recurring theme in scripture and has been a mark of faithful churches since New Testament times. If you read the whole psalm you will see how God berates figures in the council for their lack of concern for those requiring deliverance from the hand of the wicked, and he condemns them to death – they are to become 'like mortals'.

The challenge for our churches is to stand up for justice in societies where the poorest and weakest members are rarely heard. We must not allow ourselves to fall under evil influences.

'Lord, when was it that we saw you hungry or thirsty or a stranger or naked or sick or in prison, and did not take care of you?' Then he will answer them, 'Truly I tell you, just as you did not do it to one of the least of these, you did not do it to me.' (Matthew 25:44–45)

LAKSHMI JEFFREYS

A prayer for judgement

O my God, make them like whirling dust, like chaff before the wind. As fire consumes the forest, as the flame sets the mountains ablaze, so pursue them with your tempest and terrify them with your hurricane. Fill their faces with shame, so that they may seek your name, O Lord. Let them be put to shame and dismayed for ever; let them perish in disgrace. Let them know that you alone, whose name is the Lord, are the Most High over all the earth.

Consider an exciting sporting contest, an artwork that enthrals you, a song or piece of music you listen to regularly, a book you return to time and again: alongside the skill of the players, artist, performer or author there was probably significant emotion involved – what we call passion. There is an enormous difference between a factually accurate written report of an event and an account of the same incident that includes thoughts and feelings. The latter always makes a bigger impact.

There is no doubting the range and strength of emotion in today's psalm. The psalmist moves from pleading with God not to keep silent to spelling out exactly how God should deal with his people's enemies. Note that the psalmist is not simply interested in revenge and seeing the enemy destroyed, but that the enemy should know the living God against whom they have set themselves.

It is relatively easy to recite factual prayers: 'Please bless…'; 'Thank you for…'; 'I am sorry…' Passionate prayers can be a challenge, because we need to be secure in relationship before expressing emotion openly. Sometimes we fear God's judgement on us; perhaps we do not really think God cares or can do anything; it may be that we are struggling with faith in general. Our psalm offers us a model of passionate prayer. We might feel uncomfortable with the sentiments expressed but many of us will have imagined dreadful consequences for those who have hurt us. Watch any cartoon and see what happens to 'the baddie'!

Spend time in silence before God before attempting to express what you really think and feel.

LAKSHMI JEFFREYS

The joy of worship

Happy are those who live in your house, ever singing your praise. Happy are those whose strength is in you, in whose heart are the highways to Zion. As they go through the valley of Baca they make it a place of springs; the early rain also covers it with pools… I would rather be a doorkeeper in the house of my God than live in the tents of wickedness. For the Lord God is a sun and shield; he bestows favour and honour. No good thing does the Lord withhold from those who walk uprightly.

After the intensity of the first few psalms, today's is like a warm bubble bath! Psalm 84 is thought to have been sung by pilgrims on their way to the temple in Jerusalem. They express a vibrant faith in 'the living God'. They long for the temple courts and the life of holiness bestowed by God. There is a reminder that God brings blessings out of hardship, as the valley of tears (Baca) is transformed to bring water and thereby life all around. The very act of pilgrimage is holy – perhaps sacramental – as visible actions become the means of God's grace.

People have an inbuilt desire for pilgrimage, irrespective of religious faith. We have a neighbour who travels the world to watch his football team play. He makes the journey with others, anticipating the main event; they sing and eat and drink together; after it is over the details of the match are recounted incessantly, as are the adventures during travel. They have seen and lived what they would never have experienced, even on satellite television, had they stayed at home. Life is enriched as a result.

Modern Christian pilgrimage is often to Christian festivals as well as ancient places of worship. The unifying factor is the desire to gather with thousands of others to worship the living God. Such occasions, particularly if annual, provide sustenance when perhaps local individual or corporate worship is hard work. Looking back, remembering and sharing the adventures, reminds the pilgrim that he or she has experienced something life-enhancing and that the same God is with them in their daily existence.

Where do you go on pilgrimage? Whom do you worship?

LAKSHMI JEFFREYS

Prayer for the restoration of life

Restore us again, O God of our salvation, and put away your indignation towards us. Will you be angry with us for ever? Will you prolong your anger to all generations? Will you not revive us again, so that your people may rejoice in you? Show us your steadfast love, O Lord, and grant us your salvation. Let me hear what God the Lord will speak, for he will speak peace to his people, to his faithful, to those who turn to him in their hearts... that his glory may dwell in our land.

'Will you not revive us again, so that your people may rejoice in you?' Verse 6 seems to be the key verse in Psalm 85. The psalmist begins by recalling God's favour on the land – the place God prepared for and gave to his people. He restored their fortunes after they had turned away from God. Then comes the plea to do this again not simply for the sake of the people, but also so that God will be known and worshipped.

In some ways Psalm 85 is a prayerful response of people who have been allowed to go their own way (see Tuesday's comments on Psalm 81). They have realised the error of their ways and they want to live again as God intended them to, as God's people. They want what Jesus offers: life in all its fullness (John 10:10).

Of course, the life on offer here is more than mere existence. The God of the Old Testament is the living God (Psalm 84) from whom life flows. Apart from God, people perish. In addition to the land, life itself is a gift of God. This encompasses not simply breathing and daily activity, but the regular rhythms of the seasons, blessings and shalom – the peace that passes all understanding and is the hallmark of God's presence. This is life when God's glory dwells in the land.

So often our churches and Christian communities settle for existence, rather than full life. In a world where daily survival for some cannot be taken for granted, we have a responsibility to live fully and well.

Pray for people in conflict zones whose immediate goal is survival:
may God restore fullness of life.

LAKSHMI JEFFREYS

A personal complaint

A band of ruffians seeks my life, and they do not set you before them. But you, O Lord, are a God merciful and gracious, slow to anger and abounding in steadfast love and faithfulness. Turn to me and be gracious to me; give your strength to your servant; save the child of your serving-maid. Show me a sign of your favour, so that those who hate me may see it and be put to shame, because you, Lord, have helped me and comforted me.

Today's psalmist is in deep distress and significant danger. In this psalm, the speaker expresses desires and complaints to God. Yet in the middle (vv. 8–13) there is acknowledgement of God's universal glory and his works, followed by a thankful vow to live God's way and glorify God's name because of God's love. Apart from this there are 14 petitions made to God: incline your ear, preserve my life, be gracious and so on. To begin with, each request – or perhaps demand is better – is followed by a reason: the psalmist is poor and needy, is devoted to God, cries to God all day long and so on.

Another prayer of passion, today's psalm shows awareness of the nature of God. In his commentary, Marvin Tate suggests that in times of trouble there is a requirement for openness, in order to be informed by the Holy Spirit, as well as a single-minded desire to live God's way. Anyone is free to cry out to God, and God answers as God will. The person who cries out to God from a position of knowledge and understanding has the additional assurance that all shall be well, since this individual trusts God, having experienced God's love.

Apparently when I was a toddler our neighbour's daughter was in tears in her back garden one afternoon. She told me that her favourite toy had broken. 'Don't worry,' I replied cheerfully, 'my daddy will buy you a new one!' My experience of my father's generosity gave me confidence to ask and state not only my needs but those of my friend!

The better we know God in the good times, the more we can cry out in the tough times.

LAKSHMI JEFFREYS

The joy of living in Zion

The Lord built his city on the sacred hill; more than any other place in Israel he loves the city of Jerusalem. Listen, city of God, to the wonderful things he says about you: 'I will include Egypt and Babylonia when I list the nations that obey me; the people of Philistia, Tyre, and Ethiopia I will number among the inhabitants of Jerusalem.' Of Zion it will be said that all nations belong there and that the Almighty will make her strong. The Lord will write a list of the peoples and include them all as citizens of Jerusalem. They dance and sing, 'In Zion is the source of all our blessings.'

For anyone familiar with the work of John Newton, Psalm 87 brings to mind his hymn 'Glorious things of thee are spoken, Zion city of our God'. In the Bible, Zion is the city of God, the centre of life, eventually to become a dwelling place for people of all nations. In a society where belonging to a particular nation was crucial to one's identity, the psalm is extraordinarily countercultural. The few short lines express beautifully the limitless acceptance of a loving God.

The world has not changed much. In Newton's day, nations and empire conveyed belonging while racial identity meant certain people were slaves and others owned slaves. Throughout the world today there is still a craving for identity and an upsurge of nationalism, with leaders promising to make their nation great again or to build barriers and establish laws to say who is 'in' and who is 'out'.

Jesus flouted national and social boundaries, inaugurating the world in which Psalm 87 could become a reality. Anyone who accepted Jesus was accepted by him. Christians are called to model that love and acceptance, irrespective of nationality, gender or social status, since we are all one in Christ Jesus (Galatians 3:28). Called by God, we will delight together to dance and sing of the source of our blessings.

Read slowly through the psalm, then ask God to indicate countries or situations where people are not encouraged to belong. Pray Psalm 87, inserting the people God has brought to mind in place of Egypt, Babylonia and the other nations mentioned.

LAKSHMI JEFFREYS

In the pit

But I, O Lord, cry out to you… O Lord, why do you cast me off? Why do you hide your face from me? Wretched and close to death from my youth up, I suffer your terrors; I am desperate. Your wrath has swept over me; your dread assaults destroy me. They surround me like a flood all day long; from all sides they close in on me. You have caused friend and neighbour to shun me; my companions are in darkness.

It has been said that most of scripture speaks to us, while the psalms speak for us. Today's psalm is the only one in the entire psalter that apparently offers no words of hope or comfort. It is therefore essential to note that the statements are addressed to God, in the knowledge that God hears complaints. Perhaps things are so dreadful that there is nothing else to do but to cry out to God. In a society where there is always someone or something to blame, it makes sense to detail the problem to the only one who can make a difference. After all, whether or not God is directly responsible for the torrent of misery, God is allowing it to continue.

As I write, there is significant suffering due to war and famine in areas of the Middle East and in sub-Saharan Africa. There are no ready solutions or easy answers. People do not always live 'happily ever after', as fairy tales would have us believe. Perhaps the words of this psalm allow people who otherwise have no voice to realise there is a God who loves them enough to listen to their cries of anguish.

Individuals who live with depressive illnesses are often not seeking answers but long for someone to sit with them in their pit of despair and darkness. Psalm 88 does not offer any false hope or answers, but it relates the sense of hopelessness that can encompass some people. In a strange way this acknowledgement in itself can offer hope, since the sufferer is aware their feelings are shared – with the psalmist and with God. They no longer bear their misery alone.

Lord, hear my prayer.

LAKSHMI JEFFREYS

God's eternity and human frailty

So teach us to count our days that we may gain a wise heart... Have compassion on your servants! Satisfy us in the morning with your steadfast love, so that we may rejoice and be glad all our days. Make us glad for as many days as you have afflicted us, and for as many years as we have seen evil. Let your work be manifest to your servants, and your glorious power to their children. Let the favour of the Lord our God be upon us, and prosper for us the work of our hands.

Psalm 90 has echoes of Ecclesiastes and Lamentations, known as wisdom literature: recognition of the brevity and apparent futility of human existence within the love and provision of the eternal God. At the same time there are reminders of the opening chapters of Genesis. God is creator of the whole world from the very beginning; sin has led to a shortening of the human lifespan to 70 or 80 years; God is compassionate and offers steadfast love to those he created. It is as if the psalmist is crying out to God for mercy on his short-lived people so that their (our?) days have meaning and value.

The story is told of a man who realised he would not live for ever. On his 50th birthday he filled a jar with 1,300 marbles. Every Saturday he removed a marble from the jar, reckoning he had enough marbles to last until he was 75. He literally counted his weeks to ensure that every week would count. Any time he lived beyond the age of 75 would be a bonus. This approach to life cuts across a fear of death that seems to prevail: knowing that life will end, we are free to live well until it does so.

The psalmist prays that God will give wisdom and an experience of love from the beginning. This will result in thankfulness ('rejoice and be glad all our days') and the work of our hands will prosper under God.

O God, our help in ages past,
Our hope for years to come;
Be thou our guard while life shall last,
And our eternal home.
(Isaac Watts, 1719)

LAKSHMI JEFFREYS

Assurance of God's protection

Because you have made the Lord your refuge, the Most High your dwelling-place, no evil shall befall you, no scourge come near your tent. For he will command his angels concerning you to guard you in all your ways. On their hands they will bear you up, so that you will not dash your foot against a stone... Those who love me, I will deliver; I will protect those who know my name. When they call to me, I will answer them; I will be with them in trouble, I will rescue them and honour them. With long life I will satisfy them, and show them my salvation.

Whoever lives under God's protection will acknowledge God's provision. So opens Psalm 91, and it goes on to list the ways in which God will protect the psalmist from all kinds of evil and misfortune. The last three verses, quoted above, are spoken by God to us, confirming all that the psalmist has prayed. Those who trust God will experience God's protection wherever and whenever they are, kept safe by angels from physical and other attack. Praying through Psalm 91 has that 'warm bubble bath' effect on me again!

The physical dangers mentioned may be metaphors for spiritual dangers, supernatural powers of the occult, from which only God can protect us. Perhaps it is no coincidence that, when tempting Jesus in the wilderness to throw himself off the pinnacle of the temple, the devil quotes this psalm to assure Jesus that God will send angels to protect him. Jesus rebukes the devil: those who trust God have no need to put God to the test. The devil quotes a couple of verses; Jesus knows the whole psalm in context.

Understanding both what Scripture actually says and what it means in context is possible only as we pray and listen to God through the Bible. We are then, like Jesus, able to take hold of God's promises and challenge those who proof-text.

Read through Psalm 91 and allow God to show you areas of your life where he will protect you. Pray for an increased ability to trust and rely on God's protection.

LAKSHMI JEFFREYS

A song for the Sabbath day?

How great are your works, O Lord! Your thoughts are very deep! The dullard cannot know, the stupid cannot understand this: though the wicked sprout like grass and all evildoers flourish, they are doomed to destruction for ever, but you, O Lord, are on high for ever. For your enemies, O Lord, for your enemies shall perish; all evildoers shall be scattered… The righteous flourish like the palm tree, and grow like a cedar in Lebanon. They are planted in the house of the Lord; they flourish in the courts of our God. In old age they still produce fruit; they are always green and full of sap, showing that the Lord is upright; he is my rock and there is no unrighteousness in him.

The title of Psalm 92 in the Bible is 'A song for the Sabbath day'. This psalm might have been used in worship on the Sabbath, but there is nothing about Sabbath in the content. So what might be the links between God's ordained day of rest and a joyful account of what appears to be either a victory parade or perhaps a festival?

God created the world and then rested. After the exodus, God instructed Moses to institute a Sabbath. On this day there would be no work; instead God's people would be restored in relationship to God, one another and themselves. Perhaps the infusion of thanksgiving in the psalm is an indication of someone who is focused on God. The psalmist reflects on God's steadfast love and faithfulness both day and night. There is much about the works of God's hands before the psalmist speaks of those who lack wisdom and the enemies of God.

The fear of the Lord is the beginning of wisdom. Those who put God first will see the need for rest and recovery of self and relationship. The way to flourish in the faith community (temple courts, v. 14) and remain active and fruitful in old age is to take time to 'play' with God and become familiar with him. Rather than fitting mindfulness and play into an already busy schedule, perhaps try to build a life around Sabbath rest, thankfulness to God and joy.

When is your Sabbath?

LAKSHMI JEFFREYS

The once and future king

The Lord is king, he is robed in majesty; the Lord is robed, he is girded with strength. He has established the world; it shall never be moved; your throne is established from of old; you are from everlasting. The floods have lifted up, O Lord, the floods have lifted up their voice; the floods lift up their roaring. More majestic than the thunders of mighty waters, more majestic than the waves of the sea, majestic on high is the Lord! Your decrees are very sure; holiness befits your house, O Lord, for evermore.

Our final psalm in the series is again quoted in full. Walter Brueggemann describes this psalm, often referred to as one of the 'royal psalms', as public liturgy regarding the 'new kingship' of Yahweh (*Spirituality of the Psalms*, 2002). Reading Psalm 93 there can be no doubt that Yahweh is the king who gives stability to the world. There is a sense of rushing along like the roaring floods and mighty waters it describes. Our God is beyond time; having created the world, he is holy for evermore.

Not only is the world fixed – it cannot be shaken – but the same can be said of God's decrees: they are sure and trustworthy. God is more majestic than the biggest ocean waves thundering in a storm. My husband grew up near the coast and when we visit his home town we are always struck by the magnificence, enormity, power and danger of the sea. Yet the God who reveals himself to us is mightier than any of this. The very thought is mind-boggling!

In the New Testament, Jesus demonstrates his divinity during a storm at sea when he tells the waves, 'Peace! Be still!' (Mark 4:39). In fact, the phrase can be translated literally 'be muzzled', using the same word as when silencing the demons in Mark 1:25. The Lord is almighty and to be trusted. This same powerful, eternal, majestic God makes himself known to us individually and in Christian community. Ponder this and sing God's praise!

Perhaps you can find new ways to use the psalms in prayer and worship. Psalm 93 lends itself to prayer beyond words, perhaps using art or music. Try it!

LAKSHMI JEFFREYS

Acts 1—6: adventures of a Spirit-inspired community

The Acts of the Apostles is the second volume by the hand of Luke, in which he relates the high adventures of that motley band of disciples who, despite their fears and failings, took their radiant faith in Jesus to an unsuspecting world. And all this, says Luke, was because the risen Jesus gifted these faithful believers with a heavenly dose of the Holy Spirit, who pretty much knocked them off their feet when he first arrived at Pentecost and then fired them off to the ends of the earth, proclaiming the Saviour they loved so deeply.

In the next couple of weeks, which includes Pentecost Sunday, we spend time with the early chapters of the story. We will see how those first disciples were transformed from being a rather forlorn and bereft group of friends, looking up at the soles of Jesus' feet as he slipped behind the clouds in his ascension to heaven, into a formidable band of brothers and sisters who changed the world. In the reading of these stories we must hold on to one fundamental principle, which is to recognise that these early disciples were made of the same stuff as you and I. Yes, they were remarkably inspiring, and they deserve to be honoured and remembered. But throughout these narratives Luke makes clear that their lives were glorious examples of what happens when the Holy Spirit is given room to move and breathe in the life of mortals who have chosen to follow Christ.

Some would argue that such a critical time in the life of this early and vulnerable church required an extra dose of the Holy Spirit to propel it into its mission, and no doubt it did. However, we can be fairly sure that Luke would not want us simply to be admiring observers of an interesting time in history. In every story he is beckoning us in, for we too are ordinary mortals trying to follow Jesus along the perplexing pathways of this world, who need the life of the Spirit not only to find our way but also to change that pathway so radically that it resonates with the glory of God. Such pathways are filled with miracle and wonder and draw our friends and neighbours into dynamic encounters with the God who loves them.

MICHAEL MITTON

A parting gift

After his suffering Jesus presented himself alive to them by many convincing proofs, appearing to them over the course of forty days and speaking about the kingdom of God. While staying with them, he ordered them not to leave Jerusalem, but to wait there for the promise of the Father. 'This,' he said, 'is what you have heard from me; for John baptised with water, but you will be baptised with the Holy Spirit not many days from now.'

By any reckoning, the 40 days following the resurrection of Jesus were both wonderful and disconcerting. For that group of believers who had witnessed the harrowing suffering of Jesus, the news of his resurrection was utterly wonderful. However, the risen Jesus proved disturbingly unpredictable – appearing and disappearing in a most puzzling fashion. When he did make an appearance, Jesus taught his disciples about the kingdom of God, that world that, since the events of the cross and resurrection, took on a whole new meaning. In our passage today, he gives the disciples a clear instruction: stay put. Most of the Acts of the Apostles involves movement, travel and exploration. But it all begins with stillness and waiting for a precious gift.

Jesus helps them to understand this gift by referring them to an event at the beginning of his ministry. He draws their minds back to the ministry of John the Baptist, who stood waist-deep in the running waters of the Jordan sloshing water over the people. Jesus tells his disciples that something similar will happen to them, not with the waters of the Jordan but with the Spirit of God. Just as nobody could doubt they were dripping wet from the river, these disciples would know they were drenched by the river of God. Probably few really understood what this meant, but they had learned enough about Jesus by now to know that this gift would be good news, and their hearts would have been filled with eager anticipation. The life in the Spirit is not about admiring a river; it is an encounter with the water. And it often begins with stillness and waiting.

Spend some moments in quiet anticipation.
How will God release his Spirit in your life today?

MICHAEL MITTON

Last seen in a prayer meeting

Then they returned to Jerusalem from the mount called Olivet, which is near Jerusalem, a sabbath day's journey away. When they had entered the city, they went to the room upstairs where they were staying, Peter, and John, and James, and Andrew, Philip and Thomas, Bartholomew and Matthew, James son of Alphaeus, and Simon the Zealot, and Judas son of James. All these were constantly devoting themselves to prayer, together with certain women, including Mary the mother of Jesus, as well as his brothers.

Imagine how it was for Mary the mother of Jesus. She had followed her son to the cross and had guarded the tomb where he had been laid that dreadful afternoon. Nobody knows how she spent that dark weekend, but at some point she will have heard news of the empty grave, and either that news added terrible insult to cruel injury or maybe she was on the lookout for a message of remarkable hope. When she discovered he really had risen from the dead, she must have been overwhelmed with joy. Yet she would also have realised that she had no special rights to her son's life now, any more than she had during his days in Galilee. In a remarkably humble way, she now merges into the background. In his Gospel, Luke gives Mary great prominence, especially in the infancy and cross stories. But in his second volume, Mary is simply one of the disciples and she is mentioned only this one time, in today's reading. But what a wonderful mention it is: she is found in the gathering of disciples who are together in prayer waiting for the coming of the Holy Spirit. It is perhaps a great testimony to Mary that before she disappears from the rest of the pages of scripture, she is last seen in a prayer meeting.

It is likely that this became the heart of Mary's ministry. She never sought special status in the band of disciples or made claims of prominence. The lady we meet in the story of the early church is someone of admirable humility and prayer. As such, she is a most inspiring example to follow.

What inspires you about the life and witness of Mary?

MICHAEL MITTON

A gift for the outsider

'And how is it that we hear, each of us, in our own native language? Parthians, Medes, Elamites, and residents of Mesopotamia, Judea and Cappadocia, Pontus and Asia, Phrygia and Pamphylia, Egypt and the parts of Libya belonging to Cyrene, and visitors from Rome, both Jews and proselytes, Cretans and Arabs – in our own languages we hear them speaking about God's deeds of power.' All were amazed and perplexed, saying to one another, 'What does this mean?'

So the day they have been waiting for comes, no doubt in a way few of them anticipated. It is the day of the great festival of Pentecost and the followers of Jesus are packed together in a house somewhere in Jerusalem. They are praying together when all of a sudden a wind gets up, which is clearly more than a normal wind, for winds do not originate from the inside of a building. But this one does. And not only that, the disciples notice an extraordinary phenomenon that when they later come to narrate it can best be described as tongues of flame above each head. As if this is not strange enough, they then find themselves speaking in foreign languages. The windows and doors of this building are clearly open because passers-by notice the remarkable events. They must have been astonished by the forceful gale coming from within the building and the sight of men and women aflame. But the phenomenon they choose to comment on is the fact that they hear the news of God's deeds of power in their own language.

So many people today never darken the door of their local church, because they believe that what happens inside that building is of a different culture and language to their own. If they were to step inside, they believe they would feel like a foreigner. What we notice from the Pentecost story is that the disciples were given a language for the people 'outside'. It was not about getting those outside to come in. It was about empowering and equipping those inside to learn the language of the people and share God's message in their own language.

What does 'learning the language of the people' mean to you?

MICHAEL MITTON

A seeing heart

'No, this is what was spoken through the prophet Joel: "In the last days it will be, God declares, that I will pour out my Spirit upon all flesh, and your sons and your daughters shall prophesy, and your young men shall see visions, and your old men shall dream dreams. Even upon my slaves, both men and women, in those days I will pour out my Spirit; and they shall prophesy."'

Probably much to everyone's surprise, Peter suddenly becomes a most impressive preacher. Granted, in the Gospel stories we do find him as one not slow to express his mind, but after Pentecost his natural 'gift of the gab' is transformed into such eloquence that thousands are impacted by his preaching. Peter's mind is renewed by the Spirit, and no doubt scriptures that once seemed to him to be understood only by well-trained rabbis have now acquired a whole new meaning. Experiences of God's Spirit often result in a fresh insight into the scriptures.

As Peter is still glowing with the Holy Spirit, an ancient scripture ignites his heart and mind. It was a passage from the prophet Joel that once may have meant precious little to this Galilean fisherman but now is full of significance, and he can see clear evidence of this ancient scripture being fulfilled in front of his very eyes. In fact, it is the eyes that have been especially affected by the Spirit, for men, women, young, old, slaves and free now have access to a whole new kind of eyesight. From now on, insights about God and his kingdom will not be confined to the religious professionals: they will be available to every man, woman and child on this earth who is willing to see with the eyes of the heart. Prophecy is the telling of what is seen by the heart. As we know, such seeing is often clouded by our own personal hopes and fears. But Jesus demonstrated that the Spirit first drives us into the wild places of our own hearts to search us out, before sending us out in the power of that Spirit to preach good news (see Luke 4:1–15).

Lord, grant me a seeing heart.

MICHAEL MITTON

An outbreak of radical love

All who believed were together and had all things in common; they would sell their possessions and goods and distribute the proceeds to all, as any had need. Day by day, as they spent much time together in the temple, they broke bread at home and ate their food with glad and generous hearts, praising God and having the goodwill of all the people. And day by day the Lord added to their number those who were being saved.

The result of this visitation of the Spirit and the subsequent sermon from Peter was phenomenal by any standard. People had come to Jerusalem that day thinking it was just another regular festival day. But by the time they had witnessed the astonishing events surrounding the coming of the Spirit and had listened to a sermon unlike any they had heard before, they experienced a profound transformation. They discovered that there was far more to God than they had ever imagined. This God had stepped down into their world in the form of a Galilean rabbi and had opened the doorway to a full and adventurous life in this world, with the assurance of paradise beyond. Not only that, but the life of God was released wonderfully to any who should choose to receive it.

Luke tells us that around 3,000 people were impacted by the events of that day and became signed-up followers of Jesus. These included people from those varied and distant countries and cultures listed in Acts 2:9–11. Then, perhaps the greatest miracle of all happened: this disparate group of people formed themselves into a new community, the bonds of which became so strong that not only did they love to meet together in each other's homes, but also those who had much freely and gladly shared their wealth and possessions with those who had little. The gift of the Spirit birthed a new community of extraordinary generosity. Right at the start of this movement it was clear that at its very heart, it was a movement of radical love. It is a yardstick that has challenged and disturbed every Christian church and community ever since.

How radical is your love?

MICHAEL MITTON

Unfettered joy

And he took him by the right hand and raised him up; and immediately his feet and ankles were made strong. Jumping up, he stood and began to walk, and he entered the temple with them, walking and leaping and praising God. All the people saw him walking and praising God, and they recognised him as the one who used to sit and ask for alms at the Beautiful Gate of the temple; and they were filled with wonder and amazement at what had happened to him.

The Beautiful Gate was named such for good reason – it was utterly splendid and led the way into the temple, the designated meeting place with God. There was a man in Jerusalem who probably felt anything but beautiful. He was born lame, and such disability in the culture of the day consigned him to a life of begging. He could not even get to the gate under his own steam but had to be carried there, where he hoped to receive enough cash to provide food for another day of his trapped existence. Maybe there were times he would marvel at the glorious bronze doors. Maybe there were times when he wondered whether the God who was supposed to live beyond those gates could do anything for him.

Then the day came when the God whom he assumed was stuck at the far end of the great temple stepped out to the very place where he lay. And much to this man's surprise God came in the form of two ordinary-looking men who grasped him by the hand and lifted him into a beautiful world he never imagined possible. The joy of this liberation and healing was impossible to contain. What did the dignified priests and officers of that temple think when a man leapt past them shouting and hollering at the top of his voice? He may well have been followed by Peter and John, also beside themselves in dance and laughter at the surprises of God. At any moment, and in any place, the power of God can turn a world upside down, and when it does we discover the true meaning of joy.

Lord God, keep me on the look out for your surprises today.

MICHAEL MITTON

A power surge

While he clung to Peter and John, all the people ran together to them in the portico called Solomon's Portico, utterly astonished. When Peter saw it, he addressed the people, 'You Israelites, why do you wonder at this, or why do you stare at us, as though by our own power or piety we had made him walk? The God of Abraham, the God of Isaac, and the God of Jacob, the God of our ancestors has glorified his servant Jesus, whom you handed over and rejected in the presence of Pilate, though he had decided to release him.'

The dance finally comes to an end under the shade of Solomon's Portico in the temple precincts. By now a crowd has gathered at the sound of all the shouting and laughter, and those who recognised the once-lame beggar are astonished to see that he is the cause of all the commotion. Some may have caught sight of his agile figure high-kicking in the afternoon sun and marvelled at his sudden change. The focus of attention now moves to the figure to whom the man is clinging in utter delight and gratitude. Perhaps some recognised him as the fisherman who had been a follower of the notorious Jesus. They wonder how such a man could have this power to heal.

Then the fisherman speaks and asks: why all this wondering? He explains that the power that has healed this man's feet and ankles is not his power. He and John are simply servants of the one who does have remarkable power. Peter takes them right back to Abraham – this is no newfangled religious sect breaking out here; this is rooted in the God whose miracles were manifested in the great stories of faith in history, and now have broken out of history in the form of Jesus. Once again a life-changing sermon flows from the lips of Peter and many others find new freedom as a result. It is easy to settle into a rather reduced view of God and his workings. This beautiful story reminds us that at any time we may witness a divine power surge that may well disturb our well-ordered lives.

What does God's power mean to you?

MICHAEL MITTON

Proper qualifications

Now when they saw the boldness of Peter and John and realised that they were uneducated and ordinary men, they were amazed and recognised them as companions of Jesus. When they saw the man who had been cured standing beside them, they had nothing to say in opposition. So they ordered them to leave the council while they discussed the matter with one another. They said, 'What will we do with them? For it is obvious to all who live in Jerusalem that a notable sign has been done through them; we cannot deny it.'

For the man who was healed, everything about that wonderful afternoon was good news. But there were some in that crowd for whom this news was far from good. The religious leaders were doing their best to suppress the disturbing rumours that the rebel leader from Galilee was more alive than ever, despite being put to death on a cross. Peter and John are duly put in an overnight cell, and the following day they are brought before the very hierarchy that had conspired to send Jesus to Pilate and the cross. These priests interrogate Peter and John, trying to ascertain exactly how they managed to perform such a miracle. Much to the authorities' surprise, these two Galilean fishermen respond with remarkable boldness when they should be afraid. Furthermore, the priests are offended that such obviously uneducated men were doing things that only properly educated people should do. For the priests, order meant everything.

But there was one factor that changed the whole situation. They recognised that these men had been companions of Jesus. There was a Jesus quality about Peter and John that rendered useless any complaint the priests might have had about the lack of proper religious credentials. The only qualification needed was to be a companion of Jesus. It was that companionship with the risen Jesus and the empowering of the Holy Spirit that equipped these two fishermen to preach eloquently and boldly and to perform such wonders. We can reasonably suppose that these continue to be the proper qualifications for ministry.

Today is Pentecost Sunday. Pray for the Holy Spirit to empower you to share the good news of Jesus in word and deed.

MICHAEL MITTON

Heaven-storming prayer

'And now, Lord, look at their threats, and grant to your servants to speak your word with all boldness, while you stretch out your hand to heal, and signs and wonders are performed through the name of your holy servant Jesus.' When they had prayed, the place in which they were gathered together was shaken; and they were all filled with the Holy Spirit and spoke the word of God with boldness.

No charge can be brought against Peter and John and so they are released and return to hugs and cheers from the waiting disciples. The celebration quickly turns into a prayer meeting. This kind of spontaneous prayer has evidently become a regular feature of the disciples' gatherings. And it was no quiet affair. Luke tells us that they 'raised their voices to God' (v. 24), and quite likely the neighbours were left wondering what on earth was going on. The community of disciples lets rip in joyful prayer, beseeching God to give them more boldness and more miracles (vv. 29–30). These disciples are getting a taste for such things. Just as the neighbours are about to bang on the door and ask them to quieten down, they are stopped in their tracks by something like an earthquake. Inside the house there is another visitation of the Holy Spirit. Fear dissolves in that disciple community. Their prayer for boldness has been answered.

The Venerable Bede wrote of how the great Cuthbert of Lindisfarne got caught out in rough weather on the sea and, rather than cowering in the bows of the boat, he called his friends to 'storm Heaven with our prayers' (*Life of Cuthbert*, p. 57). Many of us may shy away from such extroverted and noisy forms of prayer. We worry about the whipping up of emotions and manipulation. However, embedded in our Christian tradition right from the earliest times is a form of prayer that comes from the guts and erupts in energetic intercession in the power of the Holy Spirit. Prayer is for our full humanity, not just the respectable parts of it. There will be times of deep yearning and intercession. A consequence of such foundation-shaking prayer is frequently a new confidence.

What do you feel about this 'heaven-storming' prayer?

MICHAEL MITTON

Intensity of generosity

Now the whole group of those who believed were of one heart and soul, and no one claimed private ownership of any possessions, but everything they owned was held in common. With great power the apostles gave their testimony to the resurrection of the Lord Jesus, and great grace was upon them all. There was not a needy person among them, for as many as owned lands or houses sold them and brought the proceeds of what was sold. They laid it at the apostles' feet, and it was distributed to each as any had need.

By this stage the disciples are becoming accustomed to living in a world of miracle and wonder. House-shaking prayer, tongue-speaking and miracle-working are the order of the day. Their confidence is sky high. The Jesus who had died and risen again is manifestly with them and their opponents are at a loss to know what to do about them. Such 'success' and confidence often breeds selfishness and arrogance. But today's passage tells us that all this power was definitely not going to their heads. If anything it was going to their hearts, and their hearts were opening up in remarkable generosity. They had not forgotten the new commandment of Jesus, which was all about love (John 13:34–35). The more the disciples connected with the resurrection power of Jesus, the more they were drawn into the way of love, and one of the visible signs of loving your neighbour as yourself is sharing what you have with them. When a disciple staggered out of another powerful prayer meeting, they could not bear to see a poor person without planning how to care for them.

Thus it was that this disciple community gained an early reputation for extreme generosity. They risked personal vulnerability in order to care for others. We can read endless books and listen to countless sermons on generosity, but the fact is that we only freely give when something happens in our hearts. Giving from anything less is usually motivated by guilt, not love. Any charismatic life that is not expressed in generosity has missed something vital about the Spirit.

Dear Jesus, visit my soul with Holy Spirit generosity.

MICHAEL MITTON

Deadly deception

'Ananias,' Peter asked, 'why has Satan filled your heart to lie to the Holy Spirit and to keep back part of the proceeds of the land? While it remained unsold, did it not remain your own? And after it was sold, were not the proceeds at your disposal? How is it that you have contrived this deed in your heart? You did not lie to us but to God!' Now when Ananias heard these words, he fell down and died. And great fear seized all who heard of it.

It all seemed to be going so well. Heaven had been let loose on earth and a vibrant, generous community radiated the love of God to the world around. Then disaster strikes. The God who has been found to be so wonderful appears to have a violent and vengeful side. It is arguably one of the most disturbing stories in the New Testament. Though Ananias and Sapphira have undoubtedly committed a serious offence, the punishment seems to far outweigh the crime. It feels as if we have been hurled back into the old days of the law with its bitter penalties. No wonder great fear now filled the hearts of that infant community.

And yet, there is no evidence that the sudden death of Ananias and Sapphira was a divine punishment. What we do learn from this story is that even in the heady days of such a move of the Spirit as this, and maybe especially so, we have a hideous enemy who can fill hearts with damaging darkness. The seriousness of the spiritual battle is highlighted by this story. What Luke does *not* say in this passage is that God killed this couple. It is more that the shock of what they had done was so severe that it caused their hearts to stop. It literally drained them of life. The God who is revealed in Acts is far more likely to have wept at the demise of this couple than to want to strike them down. The closer we choose to walk with God, the more our wrongdoing harms not only our souls but our health. In our journey with God, we need a good defence against Satan and a commitment to integrity.

What is in your heart today?

MICHAEL MITTON

Shadows of grace

(And believers were the more added to the Lord, multitudes both of men and women.) Insomuch that they brought forth the sick into the streets, and laid them on beds and couches, that at the least the shadow of Peter passing by might overshadow some of them. There came also a multitude out of the cities round about unto Jerusalem, bringing sick folks, and them which were vexed with unclean spirits: and they were healed every one.

Before we have time to recover from the shock of the previous story, we are now faced with another problem, which is to do with a somewhat curious practice of the healing ministry delivered by Peter via his shadow. This is not a practice in the healing ministry commended in any Christian handbook on the subject. It sounds like it sails too close to the superstitious. And yet Luke reports that many were healed simply by lying in the path of this apostle, ensuring they were touched by his shadow. Luke seems quite unperturbed by the custom, but this may be because he has spotted something. The clue is in the word he uses for 'overshadow', which is the Greek word *episkiazo*.

He uses this word on two significant occasions in his gospel: in Luke 1:35, of the overshadowing of Mary's womb by the Spirit, and in Luke 9.34, of the overshadowing at the transfiguration. In other words, we are not talking about regular shadows here! Peter was now walking so closely in the company of his master that his life was overflowing with the creative, mysterious glory of God, which poured out on those who were in his company. It is not surprising that this had such a dramatic healing effect on those he passed. Few of us can probably imagine such a close walk with God, and yet we can take heart from this story. The message is clear: that those who journey with God carry a measure of his glory that will spill over on all whom we pass, and there is no telling what these shadows of grace might achieve.

Holy Lord, as I pass through your world today,
may I cast shadows of grace on all whom I meet.

MICHAEL MITTON

The wisdom of Gamaliel

When they heard this, they were enraged and wanted to kill them. But a Pharisee in the council named Gamaliel, a teacher of the law, respected by all the people, stood up and ordered the men to be put outside for a short time. Then he said to them, 'Fellow-Israelites, consider carefully what you propose to do to these men... Because if this plan or this undertaking is of human origin, it will fail; but if it is of God, you will not be able to overthrow them – in that case you may even be found fighting against God!'

As the story of Acts progresses, the opposition from the religious authorities intensifies. But floggings and imprisonment do nothing to dampen the spirits of Peter and the disciples, who continue to preach openly about the resurrection of Jesus. In today's reading, Peter is making a defence before the Sanhedrin, and his words infuriate them, so much so that they now want not just to punish but to kill these dangerous disciples. It is at this point that a much-respected and famous Pharisee called Gamaliel addresses the situation. Gamaliel is the teacher of Saul of Tarsus (Acts 22:3), the Pharisee who will soon make his dramatic entry into the Acts story.

Gamaliel sounds a different note from the fuming Sanhedrin and succeeds in stalling them. His logic is simple – if it is of God it will succeed and if it is not it will fail – and he warns that these religious leaders may even be fighting against God himself. It is a most daring suggestion and does seem to stall his colleagues' rush to violence. Maybe it was the wisdom of Gamaliel that helped Saul be open to hearing the voice that told him that he was fighting against God (Acts 9:1–6).

We can easily settle into our convictions of what is 'of God' and what is not. Through the ages, Christianity has been plagued by those who are convinced that their way is right and will not countenance another point of view or conviction. But Gamaliel calls us into a deep and humble listening, which is particularly significant when we meet those who have different convictions from ours.

What would Gamaliel say to you today?

MICHAEL MITTON

The face of an angel

They stirred up the people as well as the elders and the scribes; then they suddenly confronted him, seized him, and brought him before the council. They set up false witnesses who said, 'This man never stops saying things against this holy place and the law; for we have heard him say that this Jesus of Nazareth will destroy this place and will change the customs that Moses handed on to us.' And all who sat in the council looked intently at him, and they saw that his face was like the face of an angel.

As we get into chapter 6, we see the emergence of a group of leaders who take on some important practical tasks that help the twelve to focus on their primary calling. Luke tells us the names of these seven leaders, the first of whom is Stephen, who is a 'man full of faith and the Holy Spirit' (v. 5). Luke wants us to be in no doubt that the practical tasks of leadership are not for the less spiritual or less faith-filled. As Stephen sets about his practical tasks, such service seems to release a ministry that includes signs and wonders (v. 8). Not only that, but when he speaks he reveals exceptional wisdom (v. 10).

Those who were intent on suppressing this Jesus movement identified Stephen as a serious threat, so they decided to haul him before the Sanhedrin. To get a guilty verdict, they drag in some people to bear false witness against him. They wait for his response and look hard at him. As they stare at him, something in his appearance changes. The only way Luke can describe this is to say that his face became like that of an angel. Presumably there was something radiant about it that suggests Stephen's mind and heart were much more concerned about the things of heaven than the machinations of his accusers. Stephen becomes the first martyr. But before he dies he sees heaven opened (Acts 7:56). At one level Stephen was just an ordinary guy with an ordinary job, and yet his heart and mind were so fixed on heaven that his face became one that radiated the smile of God.

Lord, let the light of heaven shine through me today.

MICHAEL MITTON

1 Samuel

The books of 1 and 2 Samuel form part of the collection of Old Testament books often referred to as histories. The books record the enduring love of God during a time of major change in Israel's history – the end of the period of judges and the beginning of the monarchy. After their conquest of Canaan, the Israelites formed themselves into a loose confederation of tribes with no centralised structure of government. When a crisis came, judges arose from the different tribes to lead the nation. Samuel was the last of those judges, and the first of the Old Testament books that bear his name tells the circumstances of Samuel's birth and childhood and shows how he grew up to become the one to anoint Israel's first king, Saul.

The period of the judges was an unstable time. The institution of the monarchy came about because Israel wanted more structure to their government. They wanted to be able to rely on their own organisation rather than wait for a new judge to appear from among the tribes. For the Israelites, it was a matter of being careful what you wish for. Saul was their first king. He did not obey God, so God had to choose another king, David, who would. Out of the chaos of Saul's reign comes the reign of David, the ancestor of the Messiah.

For God the Israelites' request for a king was an opportunity to show his gracious love. God remains faithful to Israel. He knew that in asking for a king the Israelites were saying 'no' to living a life of faith and they were turning their backs on their unique set-apart status as the people of God. They wanted a king in order to be like other nations. The lesson we learn from 1 and 2 Samuel is that God works through muddled, imperfect, sinful human beings. God did not want Israel to have a king but he still blessed them and they prospered. This is an encouragement to all of us as we seek to live out our lives before God.

BOB MAYO

Faithfulness in prayer

Her rival used to provoke her severely, to irritate her, because the Lord had closed her womb… She was deeply distressed and prayed to the Lord, and wept bitterly… She made this vow: 'O Lord of hosts, if only you will look on the misery of your servant, and remember me, and not forget your servant, but will give to your servant a male child, then I will set him before you as a nazirite until the day of his death. He shall drink neither wine nor intoxicants and no razor shall touch his head.'

Infertility is a hard blow for any couple. For a woman to be mocked by other women because she cannot have children is cruel. This is what happens to Hannah. Hannah does not become bitter or resentful but prays in anguish to the Lord. In many cultures childless women suffer discrimination, stigma and ostracism. In our society childless women can sometimes be pitied and not given credit the life that they have made for themselves.

This passage teaches us about the need for diligence in prayer. The Bible says that the prayer of a righteous person is 'powerful and effective' (James 5:16). There are lessons for us in how Hannah prays. Her prayers were for God's sake rather than her own. If she gave birth to a male child she would dedicate him to the Lord. The Bible says that 'this is the confidence we have in approaching God: that if we ask anything according to his will, he hears us' (1 John 5:14, NIV). Hannah's prayers were ongoing and heartfelt. She didn't expect immediate results and give up when things did not happen accordingly.

In our quick-fix society, it is easy to find ourselves being impatient when things do not happen straight away. Answers to prayers don't always happen immediately. We are told in scripture to pray continually (1 Thessalonians 5:17), and this is what Hannah does.

Hannah is determined; she doesn't give up and keeps on praying. She is also vulnerable because she is praying for something that means a lot to her. How can we learn from the example of Hannah and be both determined and vulnerable in how we pray?

BOB MAYO

God answers Hannah's prayer

Hannah prayed and said, 'My heart exults in the Lord; my strength is exalted in my God. My mouth derides my enemies, because I rejoice in my victory. There is no Holy One like the Lord, no one besides you; there is no Rock like our God. Talk no more so very proudly, let not arrogance come from your mouth; for the Lord is a God of knowledge, and by him actions are weighed. The bows of the mighty are broken, but the feeble gird on strength.'

Hannah's prayer in this passage is similar to the Magnificat, which Mary was to pray 1,000 years later (see Luke 1:46–55). Hannah and Mary both offer their prayers in response to the news that they are pregnant. They both rejoice and give thanks to God who has performed the unexpected. 'Those who were hungry are hungry no more,' says Hannah (v. 5, NIV); 'He has filled the hungry with good things,' says Mary (Luke 1:53, NIV).

Both women were in a vulnerable position. Mary, who found herself pregnant while still unmarried, was in danger because her culture emphasised family honour. Her pregnancy would dishonour the whole family, and she did not know how Joseph, her betrothed, would react. Hannah was one of two wives. Her husband Elkanah's other wife, Peninnah, had provided him with children and she mocked Hannah year after year because Hannah could not.

Hannah's prayer is an illustration of a rich biblical theme: let the one who boasts boast in the Lord (1 Corinthians 1:31). Hannah is thrilled by what God has done and she wants people to share in her good news. It is all too easy for us to have questions, doubts and uncertainty about our seemingly unanswered prayers. What about when we do see obvious changes happen in response to our prayers? How do we react then? Do we have the faith of Hannah to be able to respond with joy? It sometimes takes as much faith to accept an answer to prayer as it does to ask God in the first place or to persevere in prayer when we don't see the transformation we are hoping for.

How can we learn both to rely on God when he seems unresponsive and to rejoice in God when our prayers are answered?

BOB MAYO

Listening to God

Now Samuel did not yet know the Lord, and the word of the Lord had not yet been revealed to him. The Lord called Samuel again, a third time. And he got up and went to Eli, and said, 'Here I am, for you called me.' Then Eli perceived that the Lord was calling the boy. Therefore Eli said to Samuel, 'Go, lie down; and if he calls you, you shall say, "Speak, Lord, for your servant is listening."' So Samuel went and lay down in his place. Now the Lord came and stood there, calling as before, 'Samuel! Samuel!' And Samuel said, 'Speak, for your servant is listening.'

This is the third time that God has called out to Samuel. Samuel finally understands that it is God who is speaking. He had thought previously that it had been Eli.

The events take place at night; it is often away from the busyness of the day that we are able to hear God speaking. A recurring motif of 1 Samuel is that throughout the country's political turmoil Samuel – whose name means 'God has heard' – is the person who consistently and regularly hears God's voice. This incident in the temple shows how Samuel will live the rest of his life as a faithful servant of God.

In our society, we are encouraged to keep busy. If we want to hear God speaking, we need to learn to live our lives at a different tempo. If we pray only when we are busy, then we want God on our own terms. Isaiah 30:15 tells us, 'This is what the Sovereign Lord, the Holy One of Israel, says: "In repentance and rest is your salvation, in quietness and trust is your strength…"' (NIV).

We can learn from both Samuel and Eli. Samuel teaches us that some-times we fail to hear the voice of God. Eli teaches us that sometimes we are in a position to help a younger person with their prayer life.

How often might God have been speaking to us and we failed to recognise his voice? How can we help others to listen also?

BOB MAYO

God's presence is everywhere

The man said to Eli, 'I have just come from the battle; I fled from the battle today.' He said, 'How did it go, my son?' The messenger replied, 'Israel has fled before the Philistines, and there has also been a great slaughter among the troops; your two sons also, Hophni and Phinehas, are dead, and the ark of God has been captured.' When he mentioned the ark of God, Eli fell over backwards from his seat by the side of the gate; and his neck was broken and he died, for he was an old man, and heavy. He had judged Israel forty years.

When the old priest Eli hears the news that the ark has been captured, the shock kills him. Eli is overweight and breaks his neck as he falls backwards off the chair. Israel was a young country finding its place in the world and the Philistines threatened her with destruction. Like the Elgin marbles for Greece or the crown jewels for the UK, the ark of the covenant was key to Israel's national identity.

In the eyes of the Israelites, the ark was not simply an artefact from the past. The ark of the covenant – the chest containing the tablets of stone on which the ten commandments were written, as described in Exodus – was the actual place of God's presence. If the ark was gone then Israel was lost.

This passage teaches us the difference between the Old Testament and the New Testament revelation of God. In the Old Testament, God's revelation is written on tablets of stone. In the New Testament, God's revelation is written 'with the Spirit of the living God, not on tablets of stone but on tablets of human hearts' (2 Corinthians 3:3, NIV). In the Old Testament, God's revelation happens in specific places. In the New Testament, we each know God in our hearts and we see God wherever we look.

Today there is no need for an ark of the covenant, because 'they shall not teach one another or say to each other, "Know the Lord," for they shall all know me, from the least of them to the greatest' (Hebrews 8:11, quoting Jeremiah 31:34).

In what ways do you 'know the Lord' in your daily life?

BOB MAYO

Thinking outside the box

And there came out from the camp of the Philistines a champion named Goliath, of Gath, whose height was six cubits and a span. He had a helmet of bronze on his head, and he was armoured with a coat of mail; the weight of the coat was five thousand shekels of bronze… When the Philistine drew nearer to meet David, David ran quickly towards the battle line to meet the Philistine. David put his hand in his bag, took out a stone, slung it, and struck the Philistine on his forehead; the stone sank into his forehead, and he fell face down on the ground.

Goliath was always going to win in a straight fight. If the shepherd boy David were to stay alive and beat the giant warrior, he was going to need to think creatively. Goliath prepared for a traditional clash of arms and was going to rely on his superior size, strength and military knowledge. David was initially urged to wear armour because that was what was expected of him.

But David realised that he had a hidden advantage over Goliath: his ability to generate new solutions to conventional situations. David ignored standard practice by refusing the armour; he knew that if he fought the Philistine champion in a predictable manner he would lose. By God's grace David was able to think differently. He used his shepherd's slingshot to fell the giant.

It is an art to turn disadvantages into opportunities. Those with dyslexia succeed owing to their highly developed listening skills. Children in large classes learn to collaborate well with their peers. Older people living on their own grow to be prayer warriors.

Sometimes we might feel that we are facing a situation that is Goliath-like in difficulty. Faith in God means that we can have the confidence to try doing things differently.

How can we learn from the example of David and show creativity and imagination in how we tackle issues we face? Like David, we may need to learn that dealing with an issue head-on is not always the best thing to do.

BOB MAYO

God works through a situation that is not of his making

Then all the elders of Israel gathered together and came to Samuel at Ramah, and said to him, 'You are old and your sons do not follow in your ways; appoint for us, then, a king to govern us, like other nations.' But the thing displeased Samuel when they said, 'Give us a king to govern us.' Samuel prayed to the Lord, and the Lord said to Samuel, 'Listen to the voice of the people in all that they say to you; for they have not rejected you, but they have rejected me from being king over them... Now then, listen to their voice; only – you shall solemnly warn them, and show them the ways of the king who shall reign over them.'

The Israelites thought that a king would offer order and stability so that they could be like other countries. The difference between a king and a judge was that with a king the Israelites would know where they stood. There would be a set line of inheritance and they would know who was next in line to the throne. They would not have to wait in faith for God to choose a judge from among the tribes to rescue them from their enemies and establish peace and justice in the land.

Samuel felt that the request showed that the people lacked trust in God. When Samuel prayed about the situation, however, God told him to go ahead and allow the people to have a king. God took the Israelites' thoughts about what would give them security and used them to his glory. Saul was the first king of Israel but after him came David, who was a man after God's heart (1 Samuel 13:14). Around 1,000 years later the Messiah would be born of the line of David (John 7:42). God's plan for the redemption of the world would come through the particular circumstances of Israel's initial rejection of him and demand for a king.

This passage illustrates how 'all things work together for good for those who love God, who are called according to his purpose' (Romans 8:28).

Reflect on an occasion in your life when what seemed an initial disaster contained the seeds of good. Thank God for that time.

BOB MAYO

God works from humble beginnings

Saul answered, 'I am only a Benjaminite, from the least of the tribes of Israel, and my family is the humblest of all the families of the tribe of Benjamin. Why then have you spoken to me in this way?'... And David said, 'Does it seem to you a little thing to become the king's son-in-law, seeing that I am a poor man and of no repute?'

Saul and David were both from the bottom rung of the social ladder and exalted to kingship. They both had humble beginnings: Saul came from the smallest tribe of Israel; David was the youngest son in his family. David and Saul think of themselves as unworthy of what is being asked of them. Neither could understand why they had been chosen.

Moses had the same reaction when he was asked by God to go to Pharaoh and demand that he let the Israelites leave Egypt. Moses argued with the Lord, saying, 'Since I am a poor speaker, why would Pharaoh listen to me?' (Exodus 6:30).

In the New Testament, when Simon Peter saw the large number of fish they had caught after following Jesus' instruction, he fell at Jesus' knees and said, 'Go away from me, Lord, for I am a sinful man!' (Luke 5:8).

The heart of Christian teaching is that strength and new life come out of weakness and vulnerability. Resurrection comes the other side of crucifixion. David and Saul were faithful to God only for as long as they admitted their frailties and recognised how much they needed to rely on God for his guidance. Saul's pride and vanity meant that he did not listen to God, and in the end it cost him his kingship.

We spend a lot of our time trying to prove to others that we are competent, capable or trustworthy. If we admit our vulnerability and need of God, God's promise to us is: 'My grace is sufficient for you, for power is made perfect in weakness' (2 Corinthians 12:9).

Heavenly Father, help me to remember each day that I can't manage things on my own but need your strength and guidance.

BOB MAYO

Authenticity

Samuel said to all Israel, 'I have listened to you in all that you have said to me, and have set a king over you. See, it is the king who leads you now; I am old and grey, but my sons are with you. I have led you from my youth until this day. Here I am; testify against me before the Lord and before his anointed. Whose ox have I taken? Or whose donkey have I taken? Or whom have I defrauded? Whom have I oppressed? Or from whose hand have I taken a bribe to blind my eyes with it? Testify against me and I will restore it to you.' They said, 'You have not defrauded us or oppressed us or taken anything from the hand of anyone.' He said to them, 'The Lord is witness against you, and his anointed is witness this day, that you have not found anything in my hand.' And they said, 'He is witness.'

This passage shows the importance of authenticity and integrity. Samuel had served the Lord faithfully all of his life since his childhood. He had been the last judge of Israel and now a new era of kingship was about to begin.

Samuel knew that his position as a public leader in Israel was coming to an end but before he handed over the reins of power he wanted the people to recognise his integrity as a leader. He also wanted them to see that he had lived his whole life as an honest and authentic witness to the faithfulness of God.

Integrity is a necessary part of any leadership. Paul writes that an elder must be self-controlled, upright, holy and disciplined (Titus 1:8).

Authenticity is a quality widely admired in our society. People might mistrust those who are in authority, but they will be drawn to those whom they feel they are able to trust.

What makes for an 'authentic life'? How can we be sure that
we are being authentic in how we live our lives?

BOB MAYO

Pray for those in authority

'See, here is the king whom you have chosen, for whom you have asked; see, the Lord has set a king over you. If you will fear the Lord and serve him and heed his voice and not rebel against the commandment of the Lord, and if both you and the king who reigns over you will follow the Lord your God, it will be well; but if you will not heed the voice of the Lord, but rebel against the commandment of the Lord, then the hand of the Lord will be against you and your king.'

The book of 1 Samuel is set against a backdrop of social and political turmoil. Israel's very existence as a country is under threat. She is under attack by the Philistines and here also by the Ammonites.

God does not turn away from the Israelites. He will remain faithful to the Israelites, but only if they give their hearts to him. They have chosen to trust a king but their ultimate faith must always be in God.

In our society we tend to think of our individual behaviour and the political order of the day as separate and distinct. We do not think of our behaviour as threatening the welfare of the country, in the way that Samuel here says it does.

Samuel makes clear that the future safety of the country depends on the individual faith of the Israelites and whether they serve the Lord and obey his commands.

It is easy for us to complain and be cynical, but we have a responsibility to pray for those in power. Paul writes, 'I urge, then, first of all, that petitions, prayers, intercession and thanksgiving be made for all people – for kings and all those in authority, that we may live peaceful and quiet lives in all godliness and holiness' (1 Timothy 2:1–2, NIV).

How do we pray for those in authority?
What should we pray for local and national politicians?

BOB MAYO

Don't take people at face value

But the Lord said to Samuel, 'Do not look on his appearance or on the height of his stature, because I have rejected him; for the Lord does not see as mortals see; they look on the outward appearance, but the Lord looks on the heart'… Saul said to David, 'You are not able to go against this Philistine to fight with him; for you are just a boy, and he has been a warrior from his youth.'

In this passage God sends Samuel to anoint the new king of Israel. Samuel sees an obvious candidate and thinks that he is the person whom God has chosen, but God tells him not to judge people by their external appearance.

David is seemingly an unlikely choice for king, so it is natural for Samuel to be surprised. Even Samuel had to learn to trust God and not to jump to conclusions.

This is David's first appearance in the story. David is shown to be a courageous warrior as well as a poet and musician. (In the book of Psalms he is credited with composing many of them.) He is described as a man after God's own heart (1 Samuel 13:14).

The challenge that God gives to Samuel is as relevant today as it was then. In our society we base a lot on image and instant impressions. How do we avoid making snap judgements about people?

Don't judge a book by its cover! Jumping to conclusions is at best clumsy and at worst prejudiced.

James told the church not to give special attention to people just because they were wearing fine clothes. The church should not show favouritism to people because they appear to be wealthy (James 2:3–4). The challenge of this passage to us is how do we learn to look at people's hearts and not judge them by appearance?

Heavenly Father, help me to see through your eyes. Help me to look beyond external appearances and find the inner person. Give me a tender, non-judgemental heart that is filled with love.

BOB MAYO

The importance of friendship

When David had finished speaking to Saul, the soul of Jonathan was bound to the soul of David, and Jonathan loved him as his own soul. Saul took him that day and would not let him return to his father's house. Then Jonathan made a covenant with David, because he loved him as his own soul... Thus Jonathan made a covenant with the house of David, saying, 'May the Lord seek out the enemies of David.' Jonathan made David swear again by his love for him; for he loved him as he loved his own life..

These verses tell the story of Jonathan and David's love for each other. David grieved after Jonathan was killed fighting against the Philistines at Mount Gilboa. The strength of their friendship is shown by David's lament at Jonathan's funeral. He described his relationship with Jonathan as more wonderful than that of women (2 Samuel 1:26).

David and Jonathan could easily have become jealous rivals for the throne of Israel. Jonathan was a prince, the firstborn son of King Saul; David was the son of a shepherd. Jonathan would have expected to some day be king himself, yet Samuel tells Jonathan's father that God has chosen David to be king instead. What might have pulled Jonathan and David apart instead drew them together. They both had faith in God and a shared desire to do what was best for Israel.

David and Jonathan's friendship started when each recognised the courage in the other. Both were men of action. David had defeated Goliath; Jonathan had initiated a one-man war against the Philistines (1 Samuel 14).

Both also had a strong relationship with God: David became a man after God's heart (see Acts 13:22), while Jonathan accepted God's decision that David should be king.

David and Jonathan were not threatened by each other. Instead each admired the other. They were bound together by a shared love of God and commitment to the welfare of Israel. They thought of what was best for the other person before they thought of what was best for themselves. How can we learn to have the same attitude with our family and friends?

BOB MAYO

The dangers of jealousy

And the women sang to one another as they made merry, 'Saul has killed his thousands, and David his tens of thousands.' Saul was very angry, for this saying displeased him. He said, 'They have ascribed to David tens of thousands, and to me they have ascribed thousands; what more can he have but the kingdom?' So Saul eyed David from that day on. The next day an evil spirit from God rushed upon Saul, and he raved within his house, while David was playing the lyre, as he did day by day. Saul had his spear in his hand; and Saul threw the spear, for he thought, 'I will pin David to the wall.' But David eluded him twice.

Saul was angry when he realised that David was more popular than he was. At the same time, when he was angry he wanted David to play music to soothe him. David was both a warrior and a poet; the man who killed Goliath also wrote a number of the Psalms.

By all outward appearance, Saul was in control. He had the power. He had the throne and the army. In reality, Saul was afraid of David. This was because the Lord was with David. Saul also saw David as a threat because people thought so highly of him.

The closer David got to the Lord, the more jealous Saul became of him (1 Samuel 18:28-29). Saul did not accept God's decision that David should become king in his place and did not want to make way for the Lord's chosen one to come to the throne. Since David was going to take over the kingdom in place of Saul, it is not surprising that Saul felt as he did towards him.

How can we avoid making the same mistake when decisions are made with which we disagree? How can we learn to celebrate other people being promoted without getting jealous?

It is not unusual to be threatened by those with whom we have been close. There will always be other people more popular or clever than we are. How can we learn to celebrate other people's strengths and achievements without being threatened by them?

BOB MAYO

Waiting for God's timing

He came to the sheepfolds beside the road, where there was a cave; and Saul went in to relieve himself. Now David and his men were sitting in the innermost parts of the cave. The men of David said to him, 'Here is the day of which the Lord said to you, "I will give your enemy into your hand, and you shall do to him as it seems good to you."' Then David went and stealthily cut off a corner of Saul's cloak... Saul said, 'Is this your voice, my son David?' Saul lifted up his voice and wept. He said to David, 'You are more righteous than I; for you have repaid me good, whereas I have repaid you evil.'

When David was presented with the opportunity to sneak up and kill Saul (the very one trying to murder him), he refused because he had given his word to Jonathan that he would not harm any of his family.

David was also not going to kill Saul because he was content to wait for God's timing. He knew that God would make him king when he was ready and the time was right.

David cut off the corner of Saul's robe because he wanted Saul to know that he had spared his life. Confronted by David's clemency, Saul realises his wrongdoing in wanting to have David killed.

We are an impatient, results-driven, outcome-oriented society. People want to see things happen immediately. If a person describes themselves as having to wait for something, the assumption is that something will have gone wrong.

Waiting for the right time doesn't fit easily into a culture of now. It can feel as if we are procrastinating and putting off a decision that needs to be taken. However, waiting in faith on God is a key virtue for Christians.

God's timing is never early, and it's never been late.

Patience is a fruit of the Spirit (Galatians 5:22).
How can we learn to be patient and wait for the right time?

BOB MAYO

Serving the needs of others

Then David sent and wooed Abigail, to make her his wife. When David's servants came to Abigail at Carmel, they said to her, 'David has sent us to you to take you to him as his wife.' She rose and bowed down, with her face to the ground, and said, 'Your servant is a slave to wash the feet of the servants of my lord.' Abigail got up hurriedly and rode away on a donkey; her five maids attended her. She went after the messengers of David and became his wife.

Abigail was an intelligent and beautiful woman. She had been married previously to a man who was surly and mean in his dealings. On one occasion, she had saved her husband's life by pleading to David for clemency. When her husband died David married her himself.

The role that Abigail plays in this story helps us to reflect on the role that we play in other people's lives. Sometimes we take a prominent role and are responsible for things happening. At other times we play a supporting role and we have to be prepared to let other people take the credit. Abigail is happy to take on this latter role by telling David that she would become his servant.

The role of servant is one commanded of us all – men as well as women – for even the Son of Man did not come to be served, but to serve (Mark 10:45). The Bible says that we should serve the needs of others rather than demand our own rights.

There is a distinction to be drawn between being a servant and choosing to serve. Jesus was not a servant in the sense that he had to do what he was told whether he agreed or not. Jesus chose to serve and to put himself out voluntarily for the needs of others.

Abigail was an example of a person willing to serve the needs of others. The challenge to us is to do the same.

What might it mean to think of others before we think of ourselves?

BOB MAYO

Fate and free will in Mark's Gospel

One of the most memorable scenes of Shakespeare's *Macbeth* is that where Macbeth meets the witches who foretell his future: 'All hail, Macbeth! Hail to thee, Thane of Glamis!', 'All hail, Macbeth! Hail to thee, Thane of Cawdor!', 'All hail, Macbeth, that shalt be king hereafter!' Much ink has been expended discussing whether Macbeth is slave to a destiny that has been decided by others, but for me the tragedy of Macbeth is that although he is capable of making good choices, he chooses not to. His fate – and his ultimate downfall – lies within his own hands.

Similar questions have been raised about the role of destiny and free will in the life of Christ: was he ever given the choice of refusing his role, remaining instead a carpenter? Was Judas simply a pawn in the story of salvation, his role unfairly given to him with no option to decline it? Within the context of Mark's Gospel, however, these questions carry little significance. Mark is instead concerned with drawing from us a consideration of the nature of freedom within the love of God. He shows us the vocation of Christ and helps us to reflect on the sort of freedom this offers. We study the idea of the servant leader, and see examples of people who might consider themselves free but are in fact enslaved to material possessions, power and authority, or their own character flaws. We learn that only when we are able truly to submit to the will of God, freely and willingly letting go of our own concerns and interests and allowing ourselves to be focused wholly on those of the kingdom, only then will we experience the freedom that is offered by God through Christ's saving work on the cross. 'For whoever wants to save their life will lose it, but whoever loses their life for me and for the gospel will save it' (Mark 8:35, NIV).

SALLY WELCH

Choosing well

In those days, Jesus came from Nazareth of Galilee and was baptised by John in the Jordan… (and) a voice came from heaven, 'You are my Son, the Beloved, with you I am well pleased.'

'I am not a number; I am a free man.' For those of you of a certain generation, this will instantly remind you of that classic television series *The Prisoner*, which first aired in the late 1960s. *The Prisoner* is about individualism versus collectivism, about a man fighting to keep his identity when everyone around him is focused on removing it from him. It reminds us of the importance of names and of the effect of removing them, of reducing people to numbers – one only has to remember that the first thing that happened to prisoners in Nazi concentration camps was the removal of their name and their branding with a number. God doesn't substitute numbers for names. 'I have called you by name, you are mine' (Isaiah 43:1) – but in bestowing a name upon each one of us, he also gives us responsibility for ourselves and for our choices. We are individuals, and we can choose.

So here Jesus is, standing in the water with the crowd who press in from the Jordan banks for baptism. Here, Jesus begins his ministry, honed by years of prayer, of a growing relationship with God the Father. And he begins with an immersion in an insignificant, muddy river, a baptism from a prophet dressed in wild-animal skins who yet recognises the immensity of the task that he is being invited to undertake. Surrounded by people sorrowing over their sins, the sinless man is baptised.

Jesus is not baptised to wash away his sins – he is the Son of God and as such is without sin. Jesus is baptised to identify with us and with our sins, and to offer us a choice more precious than any other we will know, more important than any other we will make. Will we choose to follow him, to allow our wills to be merged with his, so that his will can be done through us?

Let us make our way together, Lord; wherever you go I must go: and through whatever you pass, there too I will pass (Teresa of Avila).

SALLY WELCH

Fearful choices

And the scribes who came down from Jerusalem said, 'He has Beelzebul, and by the ruler of demons he casts out demons'... [Jesus replied], 'Truly, I tell you, people will be forgiven for their sins and whatever blasphemies they utter; but whoever blasphemes against the Holy Spirit can never have forgiveness, but is guilty of an eternal sin' – for they had said, 'He has an unclean spirit.'

And so Jesus begins his ministry in the small villages on the shores of Galilee. He teaches and heals and exorcises. The kingdom of God is indeed near: people are being set free and made joyful all around. However, the Jerusalem scribes choose to interpret the saving acts of Christ quite differently. We cannot know the reasons behind their actions. Is it because they rest too heavily on their urban sophistication, and cannot help but despise this carpenter from the provinces? Is it because they fear that their own positions and assumptions are being challenged by these gifts so freely given to others so that they might be free? Whatever their reasons, we are told that they choose to interpret things quite differently. They assert with all their hard-won authority that what looks like victory is in fact deception. Behind Jesus lies the power of darkness. He is of the evil one.

Jesus' reply is harsh: stern warnings are uttered to all who 'blaspheme against the Holy Spirit'. Perhaps within this context Jesus is referring to the closed minds of the scribes, their unwillingness to accept the arrival of a new and different way to live. It should act as a stern warning to all of us who assume that we have all the answers or who are too frightened of losing our authority to be open to the authority of others.

God gets into our hearts through the places where we realise we don't know everything, through our moments of readiness to be surprised by grace. Shut down those chinks, and in the end we will be left alone in our certainties. Terrifyingly, God respects our freedom enough to say sometimes, 'Very well then, your will be done.'

Lord Jesus Christ, give me uncertainty in these certain times.

SALLY WELCH

Condemned by God?

When he was alone, those who were around him along with the twelve asked him about the parables. And he said to them, 'To you has been given the secret of the kingdom of God, but for those outside, everything comes in parables; in order that "they may indeed look, but not perceive, and may indeed listen, but not understand; so that they may not turn again and be forgiven."'

Most Christians are agreed that God wants all people to be saved. So does Jesus here really mean that he speaks in parables so that only a select few will hear – hiding his meaning from others so they might be lost in their sins? Is he deliberately calling some in, and shutting others out?

It seems unlikely that that's what Jesus was talking about. His concern was indeed to mask his meaning, but not so that the eternally damned would stay that way. Rather, he knew that what he was doing in his whole ministry was so new and so strange that many people would not be ready for it. The children of Israel would henceforth be setting out on a new journey, treading along unfamiliar paths. The destination would remain the same, but the route would be radically different. They would have to abandon their dreams of a militant Messiah, their hopes for a glorious national destiny.

This new understanding was so strange and so unwelcome that the people were not ready for it. It needed to be handled slowly and carefully. A new way of thinking would have to be tried, practised and shared, at first in whispers and by a few people. They were not ready for broadcast, these ideas of the first being last, the servant leader, a suffering Messiah, a kingdom of God that did not involve defeating the Romans. The freedom Jesus offered those first disciples was a strange new kind of freedom. These were hard truths to bear – and still are.

What aspects of faith do we find challenging to our concept of freedom?

SALLY WELCH

Salvation for everyone?

Later he appeared to the eleven themselves as they were sitting at the table; and he upbraided them for their lack of faith and stubbornness… He said to them, 'Go into all the world and proclaim the good news to the whole creation. The one who believes and is baptised will be saved; but the one who does not believe will be condemned.'

Once again we encounter a difficult saying of Christ, one that seems to allow no flexibility, no other possibilities, and that reduces our faith-world to a simple one of salvation or condemnation.

Sadly, statements like these are too often taken out of context and used as the justification for cruelty and abuse within the church, with some sections of humanity labelled as 'sinners' and therefore doomed for ever.

But those of us who believe in a God of love, who exists wherever there is love, whose purpose is that of love and whose love shines in the darkest of depths, illuminating them with the hope of new beginnings and trans-formed lives, find such simplistic judgements do not take into account the complexity of our relationship with our creator or the mystery of his sav-ing action.

Perhaps what we should reflect upon is the truth that we are all of us responsible for our own choices, that we have been given by God the abil-ity to decide for ourselves whether to accept the salvation offered to us through the death of his Son, and that it is up to each one of us to make that decision consciously and purposefully. We have been left free to reject evil and turn to Christ, but equally we have been given the freedom to reject Christ and turn away from all that he offers.

Where then might such actions lead us? Perhaps the condemnation is not that of God, whose ability to forgive is endless and infinite, but that of our own selves as we plunge into a pit of self-condemnation and despair.

Heavenly Father, let me use my freedom wisely.

SALLY WELCH

Underwhelming power

They said… 'Is this not the carpenter, the son of Mary… ?' And they took offence at him. Then Jesus said to them, 'Prophets are not without honour, except in their home town, and among their own kin, and in their own house.' And he could do no deed of power there, except he laid his hands on a few sick people and cured them. And he was amazed at their unbelief.

'Hit hard, hit first, hit often.' So went the battle cry of US Admiral William Halsey during World War II. This seems to be an effective strategy if one's aim is to overcome one's enemies. It is not, however, God's strategy.

The incarnation is striking for God's deployment of underwhelming power. This reaches its climax in the crucifixion, in the willingness of Christ to be beaten so that success could ultimately be achieved. But this is not where it begins. For, as Philips Brooks so famously wrote in 'O Little Town of Bethlehem', it is 'where meek souls will receive him still' that Christ enters in. Christ will not go where he is not wanted. He stands at the door and knocks, but it is up to us to open that door and let him into our hearts and souls.

Once again, the theme is God's respect for human freedom. It is the way of the world to try to compel. It is the way of the crucified God to beseech and encourage. We must be open to the Spirit of God, we must be willing to join in with what he seeks to achieve, before that possibility can be made a reality.

In his home town, Jesus' qualities were not recognised. The extraordinary happening that was the Son of God was not seen by those who knew him as 'the carpenter, the son of Mary'. So they missed out on the greatest adventure of them all – that of witnessing what God was doing, and joining in.

'Christ has no hands but yours' (Teresa of Avila).

SALLY WELCH

Who is truly free?

He lived among the tombs; and no one could restrain him any more, even with a chain; for often he had been restrained with shackles and chains, but the chains he wrenched apart, and the shackles he broke in pieces; and no one had the strength to subdue him. Night and day among the tombs and on the mountains he was always howling and bruising himself with stones.

It could be argued that the Gerasene is the truly free man in this story. After all, he has cast off all social restraint; he will not be bound; he follows his own path. I have heard disturbing echoes of these sentiments in the conversation of many people today: 'No one tells me what to do'; 'I am the master of my own destiny'; 'I must be myself'. But is this really the way of the cross? Is this really the best way to serve God and our neighbour, by sacrificing all thought of others so that we might indulge ourselves in a personal freedom that might ultimately damage not only ourselves but others also? Does our freedom of material consumption truly come without cost to our neighbour? Do our self-indulgent actions not have repercussions both for ourselves and those with whom we live?

In Christianity, freedom and restraint are not opposites. Rather, the tradition has always seen that you become free precisely through restraint, through discipline. Real freedom is not the ability to do whatever your impulses – your unquestioned, undisciplined, quite possibly lethal impulses – suggest from moment to moment; it is freedom to be what you were meant to be, a creature living in friendship with God and the rest of creation. A concert pianist performing some great work on stage, absorbed in the music of the moment, seems utterly free as his fingers fly across the keys, transporting us into another world. But this apparent liberty comes at the cost of years of hard work, hours of scales and exercises, dedication and self-sacrifice. So it is with real freedom: gaining it is hard work.

Lord God, your service is perfect freedom. Help me to find it so.

SALLY WELCH

Unwritten rules

One of the scribes… asked him, 'Which commandment is the first of all?' Jesus answered, 'The first is, "Hear, O Israel, the Lord our God, the Lord is one; you shall love the Lord your God with all your heart, and with all your soul, and with all your mind, and with all your strength." The second is this, "You shall love your neighbour as yourself."'

During my 20 years as an Anglican priest, my family and I have moved several times, and each move has necessitated a change of school. My older son, in particular, has attended six different schools, which has resulted in a varied, somewhat incoherent education. Recently, I asked him how changing schools so often had affected him. 'It's been hard in some ways,' he replied, 'but I have learned one thing: it's not the school rules that matter, those which are found on the website or in our note-books. It's the unwritten ones you need to learn quickly and follow closely.'

There are so many unwritten rules that surround us, some particular to our locality, others to our nationality or occupation. Choosing to follow or ignore these rules can have a significant impact on the way we relate to those around us, and the way we live our lives. For Christians, however, these unwritten rules must take second place to the two that were given to us by Jesus himself. These must be followed above all – those of loving God and loving our neighbour.

Written down, they seem incredibly simple. To live them out, day by day, on the other hand, is something that takes all our lives to learn, and even then we will never fulfil them perfectly. All we can do is decide, in faith, to keep them as an ideal, something to aim for, aware that daily we will fail, but equally aware that daily we will be forgiven our failures and permitted to try again.

'In the scroll of the book it is written of me. I delight to do your will, O my God; your law is within my heart' (Psalm 40:7b–8, NRSV).

SALLY WELCH

Possessed by possessions

He said to him, 'Teacher, I have kept all these [commandments] from my youth.' Jesus, looking at him, loved him and said, 'You lack one thing: go, sell what you own, and give the money to the poor, and you will have treasure in heaven; then come, follow me.' When he heard this, he was shocked and went away grieving, for he had many possessions.

In the 2000 film *Bedazzled*, a rather geeky IT worker, Elliot, is desperately in love with a girl who is ignorant of his very existence. His luck appears to change when he encounters a very glamorous devil, who promises to grant him seven wishes in exchange, of course, for his soul. Elliot begins a series of desperate wishes, each designed to gain him the heart of the one he loves, but each time Satan thwarts his plan, twisting his wish so that it no longer achieves what he wants it to. When he seeks the advice of a priest, Elliot is arrested and it is only in jail that he discovers that his pact with Satan is not a reality, as every soul belongs not to the individual but to God and is therefore not for sale. Elliot asks Satan to void their agreement. When Satan refuses, Elliot simply refuses to make a final wish. On being forced to do so, he wishes that the girl he loves should live a happy life. This selfless wish immediately voids the agreement and Elliot's soul is saved.

Every time we make selfish decisions, those that are designed solely to suit ourselves and not those with whom we share this planet, we risk our souls. In order to find freedom, we must first be prepared to lose it. In order to find what we most desire, we must first give up the desire for everything else. Just as the man who found the pearl of God's kingdom sold everything he had in order to possess it (Matthew 13:45–46), so we must be prepared to do the same. The rich young man allows his wealth to have first place in his heart, and so his heart is lost.

What position do possessions hold within your heart?

SALLY WELCH

The cost of dignity

People were bringing little children to him in order that he might touch them; and the disciples spoke sternly to them. But when Jesus saw this, he was indignant and said to them, 'Let the little children come to me; do not stop them, for it is to such as these that the Kingdom of God belongs. Truly I tell you, whoever does not receive the kingdom as a little child will never enter it.'

One of my favourite memories of my father is when he was shown a skateboard for the first time by my elder son. Realising very soon that he did not have the balance necessary to stand on the skateboard, my father decided that the only way he could ride the board was by sitting on it. This, of course, led to the children deciding that there was room for them to sit on the board as well, and all four spent an afternoon careering wildly down the steep drive outside the house, arms and legs in the air, laughing and shouting with joy. For my father knew the valuable wisdom that dignity is something to be worn lightly, that sharing moments of pure happiness with those he loved was worth more than his status as a serious businessman.

We are right to have a good sense of self-worth. We are right to expect the world to treat us, every one of us, with respect. But we must beware that this does not become a sense of self-importance, blocking our relationship with God. We must be free to question, to argue, to challenge not only the world that is before our eyes, but the world that lies beyond them. We must let our hearts and minds ponder the mysteries of the incarnation, and allow the wonder of salvation to penetrate deep into our hearts.

Lord, give me the gift of seeing life through the eyes of a child,
and the courage to set aside my sense of importance to glimpse
the wonder of creation.

SALLY WELCH

Freedom and stupidity

Jesus said to them, 'I will ask you one question; answer me, and I will tell you by what authority I do these things. Did the baptism of John come from heaven, or was it of human origin? Answer me.' They argued with one another, 'If we say, "From heaven", he will say, "Why then did you not believe him?" But shall we say, "Of human origin"?' – they were afraid of the crowd, for all regarded John as truly a prophet. So they answered Jesus, 'We do not know.' And Jesus said to them, 'Neither will I tell you by what authority I am doing these things.'

One of my favourite authors is Louise Penny, who takes the genre of detective fiction to new levels of sensitivity and profundity. Inspector Gamache, the subject of her books, has four sayings that 'lead to wisdom: I was wrong, I am sorry, I don't know, I need help'. They acknowledge that the speaker is aware of their human condition, and the frailty that is its inevitable companion, and is not afraid to admit this and seek the advice and help of others. Perhaps if the authorities in Mark had used these phrases, they would not have found themselves in the situation that they did.

The chief priests, scribes and elders in this passage are faced with two choices – either they risk the anger of the crowd or they risk losing their authority by admitting John's work was inspired by God. Because of their pride, they can no longer be the people they were meant to be. No doubt each of the scribes and priests began their careers longing to serve God and to teach his word, but their love for status and power began its corrupting work until they were trapped by their own prestige. Unwilling to lose face, they cannot see the truth that is gazing upon them, full of love and pity.

Inspector Gamache finds his freedom in those four phrases he uses as compass points for his investigation. We too might find a freedom from the bondage of status and self-importance in those same words.

Lord, let me make the most of my mistakes.

SALLY WELCH

Free to suffer

Then he began to teach them that the Son of Man must undergo great suffering, and be rejected by the elders, the chief priests, and the scribes, and be killed, and after three days rise again. He said all this quite openly. And Peter took him aside and began to rebuke him. But turning and looking at his disciples, he rebuked Peter and said 'Get behind me, Satan!'

Alas for Peter – famous throughout Christian circles for his habit of failing to understand what Jesus meant for so much of the time, pitied for his lack of insight, scorned for his cowardice. Yet he was not the only disciple to fail to grasp that Jesus the Messiah was not Jesus the military man, not Jesus the armed conqueror. Peter is not the only Christian who has found the concept of servant leadership challenging, particularly in the way that it supports encouragement and understanding over force and dogmatic assertion. These issues still present challenges to us today, but fade into comparative insignificance beside the concept that the suffering that Jesus underwent was part of God's plan for him, a plan to which he consented willingly. Only by undergoing such torment could the will of God be carried out – was it for this alone that Jesus was born?

How could an all-loving God allow this to happen? Why was the only path to the salvation of humankind a path marked by terrible pain and torment? This is a mystery which perplexes and disturbs, a truth that we may never understand this side of the grave. All we can know is that the suffering and death of Christ on the cross was inspired by, driven by and infused with a love so strong that even when the suffering was at its greatest, love reached down and gave the care of a mother to a disciple, promised paradise to a criminal suffering alongside, and begged forgiveness for those who sought to destroy love even as they tried to do so.

'No one has greater love than this, to lay down one's life for one's friends' (John 15:13).

SALLY WELCH

Radical unfreedom

They began to be distressed and to say to him one after another, 'Surely, not I?' He said to them, 'It is one of the twelve, one who is dipping bread into the bowl with me. For the Son of Man goes as it is written of him, but woe to that one by whom the Son of Man is betrayed! It would have been better for that one not to have been born.'

Did Judas have any real choice in betraying Jesus, or was he 'the one destined to be lost' (John 17:12)? Was Tim Rice right in *Jesus Christ Superstar* to have Judas cry to God, 'I'll never know why you chose me for your bloody crime?' If I were to ask you who your favourite disciple was, I would expect to hear all sorts of different names – Peter, perhaps, or Matthew, Mary Magdalene or one of the post-resurrection disciples, such as Barnabas and Timothy. I would be surprised indeed if you told me that Judas was your favourite. And yet he exerts a strange fascination for all of us, as we struggle to understand why he acted the way he did, what brought him to the decision to betray Jesus for a handful of silver, thus unknowingly earning the contempt of Christians for centuries to come.

Perhaps Judas fascinates because he is the most human of characters. Perhaps we all recognise deep within ourselves the potential for evil that is revealed in Judas, the movement towards the dark, the deliberate rejection of the good and the light. The gift of freedom, given so generously and so unsparingly to us by our creator, is precious and fragile and holds within it the potential for the greatest good and the greatest evil. Throughout the event we know as the last supper, Judas is offered again and again the opportunity to choose rightly, to reject evil, to accept forgiveness. He does not, and that is his tragedy.

Imagine again the musician deliberately choosing to hit the wrong notes: that is what Judas does with his life, and it is catastrophic. This is what radical unfreedom looks like.

Father, rescue all who are lost in the folly of unfreedom.

SALLY WELCH

Struggle and freedom

He took with him Peter and James and John, and began to be distressed and agitated. And he said to them, 'I am deeply grieved, even to death...' And... he threw himself on the ground and prayed that, if it were possible, the hour might pass from him. He said, 'Abba, Father, for you all things are possible; remove this cup from me; yet, not what I want, but what you want.'

How real was the struggle in Gethsemane? Was there ever the possibility that Jesus might have said to himself, 'Actually, no. I'm not going to drink the cup. I am going to follow a different path, one which allows me to escape and survive.'

Christian theology generally has said that there cannot have been that kind of titanic moral struggle within Jesus. He was, after all, the one whose essence was love – that is, the incarnate second person of the Trinity. God incarnate cannot really struggle about whether to accept the will of God – that would be divine incoherence. Jesus' freedom is not really a matter of choice. Freedom is the ability to be what we are – in Jesus' case, the incarnation of God. There is a certain effortlessness about freedom, about vocation embraced to the extent that alternatives have long since died away. This is often seen in those who stand up against unjust regimes, or who refuse to undertake criminal actions. It can be witnessed in more domestic circumstances, in those who refuse to take the easy way out but instead admit to their errors, apologise for their mistakes, forgive those who have insulted them. These people are driven by the knowledge that although their proposed actions will be difficult and unpleasant, they are unavoidable, because they are right, and these people have chosen the right, whatever the cost.

Similarly, we must not minimise the cost of Jesus' decision. Pain and terror and risk are the price of his freedom. No struggle, no choice, but still great sacrifice.

What is our definition of perfect freedom?

SALLY WELCH

Bound freedom

As soon as it was morning... they bound Jesus, led him away, and handed him over to Pilate. Pilate asked him, 'Are you the king of the Jews?' He answered him, 'You say so.' Then the chief priests accused him of many things. Pilate asked him again, 'Have you no answer? See how many charges they bring against you.' But Jesus made no further reply, so that Pilate was amazed.

There can be few more tragic phrases than that in Mark 15:15 describing the motivation of Pilate in determining to have Barabbas released and Jesus crucified: 'wishing to satisfy the crowd'.

What a lifetime of tragedy, of wrong choices, of a good human being distorted and twisted into the crowd-pleasing, insecure, status-obsessed official that is Pontius Pilate. Doomed to have a place in history as the one who condemned the Saviour of the world to death, he is the perfect example of the free man who is yet bound tightly in chains of his own making, unable to fulfil his God-given potential, trapped by his fear, perpetually diminished. Just as Gollum in Tolkien's *The Lord of the Rings* has been reduced to a thin, wretched creature through his longing to possess the ring ('my own, my precious'), so Pilate's political ambitions and need for power have reduced him to little more than a puppet, pulled by the strings of public opinion.

The man who stands before him, a prisoner, bound and beaten, is yet more free than Pilate can ever be. And this is the point to which Mark brings us – the recognition that true freedom is not a physical state. It is a recognition, ironically, of complete dependence upon a greater authority and a willingness to submit to that authority, whose name is love, whose gifts are greater and more precious than any that can be achieved on earth, yet freely available to all who ask.

What is the difference between heavenly and earthly freedom?

SALLY WELCH

Mountains and rooftops in the Bible

Mountains fascinate and attract us. Most of us know the thrill of reaching a summit and rejoicing in the view that it reveals. The delights of the rooftop are probably less familiar. While a rooftop is closer to earth than a mountaintop, it is usually less accessible. Perhaps this makes our 'rooftop moments' all the more memorable.

I once stayed with friends in Prague, on the top storey of a medieval building in one of the city's oldest streets. From my window I looked straight into the face of the cathedral clock and also over countless time-weathered rooftops, spread like a benevolent canopy over the old town. Since then I have always been entranced by the sight of rooftops, so it has been a privilege to explore some 'summit experiences' in scripture, whether from the top of a mountain or the top of a roof.

This scriptural exploration has helped me to understand better the spiritual implications of these high places. Both mountaintops and rooftops can offer inspiration, raising our hearts and minds to realities beyond ourselves. But both can also lead us into temptation, by seducing us into thinking we can look down on the earth, or on each other, and possess and control what we see. David gives in to such temptation; Jesus resists it.

Sometimes an extreme location is needed to help us express extreme emotion. Our own glimpses of glory in the created world or in each other are pale reflections of Jesus' mountaintop transfiguration. Our own cries of despair are echoed in the lonely bird on the rooftop, whose cries rend the night air.

And always there is the requirement to come down from the high place and return to the demands of life in the valley of everyday experience. Jesus knows this to be true as he comes down from the mountain of transfiguration. We may resist the call back to daily life, preferring to stay on the heights, but often enough life will make sure that we descend, by 'letting us down'. The story of the healing of the paralytic assures us that the 'letting down' may be the very thing that brings us closest to Jesus.

Enjoy this journey to the heights and back down again, and may God be your guide.

MARGARET SILF

The sound of silence

He said, 'Go out and stand on the mountain before the Lord, for the Lord is about to pass by.' Now there was a great wind, so strong that it was splitting mountains and breaking rocks in pieces before the Lord, but the Lord was not in the wind; and after the wind an earthquake, but the Lord was not in the earthquake; and after the earthquake a fire, but the Lord was not in the fire; and after the fire a sound of sheer silence.

Mountains have always challenged human beings to reach for the skies, as though this might bring us closer to the heavens. Even now, in the 21st century, when we have probed the galaxies and walked on the moon, many people still imagine the skies as being the dwelling place of God. Today's reading takes us to a mountaintop, to reveal the sacred presence in an unexpected way.

Elijah senses a call to go to the mountaintop and open himself to the presence of God. It probably doesn't surprise him that the mountain is named as the appropriate location for this encounter, the place at which he will get to witness the passing-by of the Lord himself.

We can imagine him alone on these exposed and dangerous heights. The drama begins as we too might have expected it, with a rock-splitting hurricane. But even the power of such overwhelming natural force cannot contain the living God. Next comes an unrelenting firestorm. But no raging inferno can hold or express the sacred fire of God's heart.

And then the long-awaited moment. Elijah almost misses it, because it comes clothed in the sound of sheer silence. If we could imagine God's word resounding through this silence it might be: 'Elijah you seek me in the drama and the power, but I am deep in your own heart, in your own deepest silence. Only in the silence will you hear my presence. Meet me there.'

We too are invited to meet the living God deep in the silence of our own hearts, a silence which is all too easily ignored amid the clamour of our lives.

May we know the great gift of 'sheer silence', if only for a few moments of each busy day.

MARGARET SILF

The heights of peace

In days to come the mountain of the Lord's house shall be established as the highest of the mountains, and shall be raised up above the hills. Peoples shall stream to it, and many nations shall come and say: 'Come let us go to the mountain of the Lord, to the house of the God of Jacob; that he may teach us his ways and that we may walk in his paths.' ... they shall beat their swords into ploughshares, and their spears into pruning-hooks; nation shall not lift up sword against nation, neither shall they learn war any more.

The medieval Japanese mystic Ikkyu reminds us that many paths lead from the foot of the mountain, but at the peak we all gaze at the single bright moon. Today we hear how the paths of all the nations gradually converge at the peak of the highest of the mountains, which rises above all other hills and is honoured as the very dwelling place of God.

We are pilgrims, each following our own unique path to that peak, but today we learn something of what this journey asks of us. It is a journey focused on peace, leading to a point at which humankind will cease to prepare for war. Those things that so far have been directed into armed conflict – the sword and the spear, both designed to destroy life – will be transformed into farming implements – the plough and the pruning shears, designed to nourish and cultivate life in its fullness.

When we begin to see these changes happening, we will know that we are getting a little closer to the mountaintop of the eternal presence of God. Dare we hope for such a transformation? In the aftermath of World War II, German civilians, starving and destitute after the bombings, learned to turn military helmets into colanders and tank tyres into shoe soles. Such are the signs that are promised by the prophet today.

Just small changes in attitude, a re-directing of human energies away from conflict and towards life-affirming activity, can be the first subtle signs of the radical transformation into which the Gospel calls us – the first glimpse of that one bright moon.

May our only arms race be a race to reach out our arms to each other in love and compassion.

MARGARET SILF

On the holy mountain

The wolf shall live with the lamb, the leopard shall lie down with the kid, the calf and the lion and the fatling together, and a little child shall lead them. The cow and the bear shall graze, their young shall lie down together, and the lion shall eat straw like the ox… They will not hurt or destroy on all my holy mountain; for the earth will be full of the knowledge of the Lord as the waters cover the sea.

This familiar description of the mountain of the Lord may sound idealistic, to say the least. Impossible to imagine such a setting, where sworn enemies within the natural world, including human beings, should become amicable; where the fierce competition between different creatures in the struggle for food, space and power might yield to a society based on co-operation rather than conflict. What could it possibly mean for us today, saturated as we are with daily reports of bitter conflicts?

Ironically, the occasional glimpses of what such a society might look like usually happen in times of great hardship or serious danger, rather than times when everything is going smoothly. Recall a disaster that you have witnessed, or any other moment when the normal running of life was frozen for a few hours, such as after a natural tragedy or violent attack, and you may also remember that in that time it didn't matter whether the dead and injured shared your ethnicity, creed or outlook on life. It mattered only that they needed help. There were heroic and selfless individuals who instead of fleeing from danger ran straight into it to help others. There were emergency workers who struggled to save the life even of the person who had caused the emergency.

Perhaps these moments are a brief foretaste of the way things shall be when we come to the fullness of our journey into God, when we truly become the people God created us to be, called to dwell on the holy mountain.

---

*Every time we choose to reach out in peace to another,
we take a step closer to the holy mountain.*

MARGARET SILF

Mount Temptation

Again, the devil took Jesus to a very high mountain and showed him all the kingdoms of the world and their splendour; and he said to him, 'All these I will give you, if you will fall down and worship me.' Jesus said to him, 'Away with you, Satan! for it is written, "Worship the Lord your God, and serve only him."' Then the devil left him, and suddenly angels came and waited on him.

The mountaintop raises our hearts and minds towards God, but it also takes us to a place where there is nowhere to hide from ourselves. To be on a mountain peak is to see the world from a different perspective, to catch a breath-taking view that is visible only at this great height. But it is also a place where we may meet our demons as well as our angels, the worst within us as well as the best.

Jesus does not hesitate to enter into this experience with us, as he goes through his own encounter on the mountain of temptation. Just as we see great views from the mountaintops, so Satan gives Jesus a panoramic view of all that could be his, if he will simply bow to Satan's rule. All the kingdoms of the world lie within his grasp, but Jesus knows the price of such a conquest, and he knows too that such power is never of God.

To rise to the heights and open ourselves to inspiration is one thing. To look down from those heights and delude ourselves into thinking that we can own, control or conquer what we see is quite another. Height can inspire us. It can also seduce us.

Yet once the temptation is resolutely resisted, the devil leaves in a hurry, recognising his ultimate powerlessness, and the angels, our trustworthy spiritual companions, return. The worst in us is thwarted when the best in us surrenders to the power of a loving God.

May we have the grace to recognise when we are being invited by God to rise to the best we can be, and when, intoxicated by our own self-importance, we are being seduced by the worst that is in us.

MARGARET SILF

Transfiguration light

Six days later, Jesus took with him Peter and James and his brother John and led them up a high mountain, by themselves. And he was transfigured before them, and his face shone like the sun, and his clothes became dazzling white. Suddenly there appeared to them Moses and Elijah, talking with him... While Peter was still speaking, suddenly a bright cloud overshadowed them, and from the cloud a voice said, 'This is my Son, the Beloved, with him I am well pleased; listen to him!'

I well remember a day in England's Lake District, when we were visiting with friends from overseas and staying in a cottage in one of the small villages there. They were eager to see the beauty of this part of the country, and we were just as eager to show them. We planned a day's hiking, involving a steep climb up one of the many Cumbrian mountains.

The next morning, however, the land was hidden under a blanket of dense fog. We couldn't even see the garden gate, let alone the mountain we planned to climb. We almost abandoned the expedition, but in the end we decided to set out, regardless of the weather. Against our better judgement we began our climb, stoically placing one foot in front of the other.

And then, after several hours' hard climbing, a miracle happened. We found ourselves above the cloud level and were suddenly and unexpectedly bathed in brilliant sunlight, gazing down on the cloudscape beneath us. The day was utterly transfigured.

There are transfiguration moments in our own lives. Sometimes an ordinary grey day can be transformed into one of startling beauty, even by something as simple as a loving word or a kindly gesture. The fogs through which we stumble can dissolve, revealing the deep truth that love, kindness and compassion are, like the sun, a permanent presence, and only the clouds of our fears, resentments and inner blindness obscure this reality from our sight.

May our hearts be open to glimpse the eternal reality of love, truth and beauty, when these transfiguration moments break through the clouds of our fears, sorrows and despair.

MARGARET SILF

Love feast

On this mountain the Lord of hosts will make for all peoples a feast of rich food, a feast of well-matured wines, of rich food filled with marrow, of well-matured wines strained clear. And he will destroy on this mountain the shroud that is cast over all peoples, the sheet that is spread over all nations; he will swallow up death for ever... Let us be glad and rejoice in his salvation, for the hand of the Lord will rest on this mountain.

Through the years of my life I have been fortunate enough to enjoy many feasts of rich and varied food, often from regions of the world that were strange to me. Sometimes these exotic dishes were even accompanied by 'well-matured wines strained clear'. By way of healthy balance, however, there have also been frugal times, when food was scarce or rationed, as in the aftermath of World War II. For all of these, the famines and the feasts, I am grateful to the Lord of the mountain. Such nourishment keeps us physically alive, keeps death at bay, but does it really destroy death for ever?

There were particular feasts that were much less impressive yet infinitely more memorable: winter afternoons after school, when my mother and I made toast together with an old-fashioned toasting fork held close to an open fire; evenings when we patiently baked potatoes in the hot centre of that same fire and then ate them with salt and a dab of butter; bowls of hot soup thick with fresh vegetables, shared with friends on cold nights, and home-baked bread straight from my grandmother's oven.

I ask myself, on reflection, what it was that made these humble meals so much more memorable than any of the more elaborate offerings. The answer is simple: the difference was in the love with which they were prepared and shared. It is love, and love alone, that lifts the shroud that overshadows our earthly existence, love that banishes the greed, fear and bitterness that deaden our hearts and our communities. A meal becomes a feast when its active ingredient is love.

Famine becomes feast, and death gives way to life,
wherever the hand of love comes to rest.

MARGARET SILF

Leaving the mountain

The Lord our God spoke to us at Horeb, saying, 'You have stayed long enough at this mountain. Resume your journey, and go into the hill country of the Amorites as well as into the neighbouring regions... See, I have set the land before you; go in and take possession of the land that I swore to your ancestors, to Abraham, to Isaac, and to Jacob, to give to them and to their descendants after them.'

Another unforgettable peak in my own family's story is Cathedral Peak in the Drakensberg mountains of South Africa. It was there that our daughter married her South African husband in a tiny chapel on the mountainside. Unknown to us, the young couple had arranged a surprise helicopter ride for the two sets of parents and immediate family, to take us up to the high plateau at the summit.

As I stood up there, in stunned silence, gazing at the amazing beauty of the vista spread out below us, where the great folds of the mighty 'Berg' stretched in all directions and a glorious sky arched above us, as if hand-painted by the great Creator, I remember thinking, 'I don't ever want this moment to end. I don't ever want to go down to the valley again.'

But the helicopter was waiting. Down in the valley there was still a wedding to celebrate, guests to greet, the newly-weds to bless with our love. We had stayed long enough at this mountain. It was time to continue our life journey on the path that lay waiting for us all.

From time to time we will experience the glory of the mountaintop experience in our lives. But the seeds of grace that are planted in our hearts at such times must be sown down in the soil of our everyday valley living, where their fruits may become a blessing to many.

As we return, perhaps reluctantly, to the valley, we may feel we are losing something precious. In reality we have been given a unique and eternal treasure, which we will never again lose, wherever the valley path may take us.

May we have the courage to live out in the valley the glory
we have glimpsed on the mountaintop.

MARGARET SILF

Place of shelter

'Go out to the hills and bring branches of olive, wild olive, myrtle, palm, and other leafy trees to make booths, as it is written.' So the people went out and brought them, and made booths for themselves, each on the roofs of their houses, and in their courts and in the courts of the house of God, and in the square at the Water Gate and in the square at the Gate of Ephraim. And all the assembly of those who had returned from the captivity made booths and lived in them.

It isn't always easy to climb a mountain. It might be rather easier to go up to the rooftop instead. The rooftop is perhaps a more accessible and homely image of the 'high places' of our hearts and souls.

Today's reading describes the Feast of Tabernacles, or Sukkot, in which the people of Israel celebrate their thanksgiving to the God who sustains them. They do this by creating little booths or makeshift huts, where they live and take their meals during the festival. These flimsy booths serve as reminders that once, in the wilderness, they lived from hand to mouth, trusting entirely in God's providence to supply their daily needs. The booths were constructed in homes and gardens using leaves and branches to form a temporary shelter, but in today's reading we discover that they were also sometimes established on the rooftops.

A rooftop shelter is a beautiful image. It brings to mind those rooftop gardens we sometimes see in the middle of built-up cities. They can usually only be seen from above – an aerial view; from street level they may be invisible. Our hearts' gardens are also a bit like that – sanctuaries of inner peace where we can reconnect to God's presence within us and around us, offering our own thanksgiving for all that energises and sustains us. They may be invisible to those around us, seen only by God, but they are our own way of acknowledging that God is the source of all that gives us life – our own way of celebrating the Feast of Tabernacles.

May we never forget our dependence on divine providence
or neglect the need to give thanks in our own way, for the gift
of all that holds us in being.

MARGARET SILF

Place of lamentation

For my days pass away like smoke, and my bones burn like a furnace. My heart is stricken and withered like grass; I am too wasted to eat my bread. Because of my loud groaning my bones cling to my skin. I am like an owl of the wilderness, like a little owl of the waste places. I lie awake; I am like a lonely bird on the housetop.

Today's rooftop is no place of celebration or thanksgiving, but a place of grief and heartache. As is often the case, the psalmist's language is extreme, to express the extremity of his soul's anguish. Indeed, such psalms of sorrow and lamentation are a God-given vehicle to carry our personal grieving and put it into words, which we know have been used all through the ages, and are still used daily in the offices of the church.

A friend of mine, following the tragic premature death of a beloved child, told me that she sometimes needed to go out to the hills of the neighbouring countryside and seek out a solitary place. There she would scream her pain to the skies, rather like the 'owl of the wilderness', but just a human soul pouring out her heart's agony into the 'waste places'.

At times like these our hearts themselves feel like the 'waste places'. Intense grief such as my friend's is far more than a state of mind that will eventually pass. It is a physical torment that seems to wrench us apart in our deepest reaches. The days pass almost unnoticed because time has lost its meaning and sleep eludes us utterly. We have no appetite either for food or for life. We burn in our pain while at the same time freezing in our helplessness to relieve it. Everything that once gave us joy and a reason to get up in the morning has withered away. Our heart's singing has turned into an unspoken, yet unbroken groan.

We can really identify with that lone bird on the rooftop in the dark of a night that seems to promise no new dawn.

May the God of all compassion hear the cries of our hearts when we have no words with which to express our grief and loneliness.

MARGARET SILF

Place of desperation

Because Ar is laid waste in a night, Moab is undone; because Kir is laid waste in a night, Moab is undone. Dibon has gone up to the temple, to the high places to weep; over Nebo and over Medeba Moab wails. On every head is baldness, every beard is shorn; in the streets they bind on sackcloth; on the housetops and in the squares everyone wails and melts in tears… My heart cries out for Moab; his fugitives flee to Zoar, to Eglath-shelishiyah.

I hope and pray that the kind of personal anguish evoked by the image of the lone bird on the rooftop from yesterday's reading is not an experience that you have known very often, or at all, in your own life. Yet grief strikes us all at some point in our lives and the psalmist helps us express feelings and reactions to which we could otherwise not give any coherent form.

Far more likely and more common is our need to express our reaction to events occurring in the world around us. This is as true in our time, where every day seems to bring new reasons to cry out in despair, as it has ever been. In today's reading it is a prophet's wisdom, rather than the psalmist's, that guides our response.

While the names of the places mentioned are probably unknown to us, it would not be hard to substitute names and places from this week's newscasts or newspapers. Mosul is laid waste in a night, and Syria is undone. A hundred thousand refugees resort to the temple or the mosque or the cathedral to weep over the bodies of their children. From the squares and the streets and the rooftops rises the wailing of the afflicted, fleeing from bombs and brutality and the ravages of conflict and natural disaster.

We watch helplessly as a million migrants flock to safer shores and our hearts, too, cry out for them. Yet not quite helplessly, because the God of compassion sends out an echoing call to our hearts: 'Remember what love asks of you in the face of all this need and human desperation.'

May our hearts never be closed against the desperate cries
of our brothers and sisters in their hour of need.

MARGARET SILF

Place of temptation

It happened, late one afternoon, when David rose from his couch and was walking about on the roof of the king's house, that he saw from the roof a woman bathing; the woman was very beautiful. David sent someone to inquire about the woman. It was reported, 'This is Bathsheba, daughter of Eliam, the wife of Uriah the Hittite.' So David sent messengers to fetch her, and she came to him, and he lay with her... The woman conceived; and she sent and told David, 'I am pregnant.'

So far this week we have seen the rooftop as a place of celebration, of reflective withdrawal, and of lonely anguish and lament. Today we discover a rather more sinister use for a rooftop – as a place to spy on what is going on in the world below, a place from which to plot evil or, at the very least, a place of possible temptation.

For David, in today's reading, an essentially innocent stroll on the rooftop becomes the gateway to temptation which will ultimately have lethal consequences. So quickly can our best deteriorate into our worst. It begins with a chance glimpse, initially unintended, of the beautiful Bathsheba bathing. We are often told that there is no sin in observing a situation or experiencing the feelings that it evokes in us, but only, potentially, in the way we react to that situation or act on those feelings.

This is where the slippery slope begins for David. He cannot control his urge to possess the beautiful woman he has seen. She is sent for and seduced. Seduction has consequences. She becomes pregnant. Now David has quite another problem. As we learn later in the story, he now has to deal with Bathsheba's husband, Uriah, who is serving with the military. Uriah is therefore dispatched to the front, in the certainty that he will be killed in battle. A passing attraction has degenerated into an adulterous liaison, which has in turn led to a murderous plot and the death of an innocent man.

From the vantage point of height we can discover our highest potential or sink to the worst we can be. May we recognise the downward spiral of temptation before it is too late.

MARGARET SILF

Place of proclamation

Meanwhile, when the crowd gathered in thousands, so that they trampled on one another, he began to speak first to his disciples, 'Beware of the yeast of the Pharisees, that is, their hypocrisy. Nothing is covered up that will not be uncovered, and nothing secret that will not become known. Therefore whatever you have said in the dark will be heard in the light, and what you have whispered behind closed doors will be proclaimed from the housetops.'

A story is told of a woman who was a notorious gossip. Whenever she had a chance she would quietly whisper some secret details about her neighbours to anyone who would listen. Each time she would emphasise that the information was confidential and must not be passed on, but, of course, every time it was passed from one set of ears to the next.

Eventually the village elder decided that it was time to put a stop to this. He called on her and pointed out that the gossip she was passing on was harmful and sometimes not even truthful and that it must stop. She was indignant and denied all wrongdoing. To convince her, the elder asked her to fetch a pillow, bring it upstairs and shake it out of the bedroom window. Immediately all the feathers in the pillow scattered in all directions; it was, of course, impossible ever to gather them in again.

'So it is with words of gossip,' said the elder. 'You whisper them in secret, but they spread all over the village and there is no end to the harm they can do. They are like the yeast in the dough. You can't see them, but they affect everything.'

In today's reading Jesus warns us about this kind of destructive 'yeast', and reminds us that nothing is ultimately secret. All is known to the heart of God. In our world today, where the line between truth and falsehood is increasingly blurred and where hidden agendas dominate decisions of national and global importance, this warning has never been more timely or necessary.

May everything we speak, think or repeat be transparent, loving and true, so that it will not bring shame when it is exposed to the light of God's truth.

MARGARET SILF

Place of enlightenment

About noon the next day, as they were on their journey and approaching the city, Peter went up on the roof to pray. He became hungry and wanted something to eat; and while it was being prepared, he fell into a trance. He saw the heaven opened and something like a large sheet coming down, being lowered to the ground by its four corners. In it were all kinds of four-footed creatures and reptiles and birds of the air. Then he heard a voice saying, 'Get up Peter, kill and eat.' But Peter said, 'By no means, Lord; for I have never eaten anything that is profane or unclean.' The voice said to him again, a second time. 'What God has made clean you must not call profane.'

Peter has discovered that a rooftop is a good place to go and pray. He is not without his troubles. The early people of the Way have disagreements about how the embryonic church should be governed and what should be required of converts. In particular, there are disputes about how far the Judaic dietary requirements should be imposed upon Gentiles.

Peter's rooftop vision may strike us as bizarre, but sometimes God uses startling and unexpected ways to break through our assumptions and shake us free when we get set in our ways. At first Peter is far from receptive. He thinks he knows best what is clean and what is unclean, and quite possibly his assumptions extend beyond the food to the converts themselves, though he would probably not admit this even to himself. He needs to fall into the darkness of a trance in order to get a glimpse of divine enlightenment.

It isn't just Peter, however. We all tend to assume that others should conform to the way we do things ourselves, and we also like to think we know best – better even than God – how matters should be conducted. Perhaps God also speaks most clearly to us when our own imagined certainties are suspended. Two thousand years later we still have so much to learn from this encounter between Peter and his God.

May we too, like Peter, learn to trust the guidance of God,
especially when it challenges our own assumptions and traditions.

MARGARET SILF

Letting down, rising up, moving on

When he returned to Capernaum after some days, it was reported that he was at home. So many gathered around that there was no longer room for them, not even in front of the door; and he was speaking the word to them. Then some people came, bringing to him a paralysed man, carried by four of them. And when they could not bring him to Jesus because of the crowd, they removed the roof above him; and after having dug through it, they let down the mat on which the paralytic lay. When Jesus saw their faith, he said to the paralytic, 'Son, your sins are forgiven.'

Today's reading, the last of our reflections on mountaintops and rooftops, takes us to one of my favourite New Testament stories. It begins with an overwhelming desire on the part of so many people to get a glimpse of Jesus and be touched by his healing power. The desire is so insistent that people have gathered in their multitudes outside his home in Capernaum.

But their determination is nothing compared to that of the paralysed man and his friends, who, finding all access barred, apply themselves to finding more ingenious ways of getting their sick friend to the Master. The rooftop provides the way to the feet of the Lord.

The details provided by Mark leave us with the impression of a major construction – or de-construction – project, as they physically remove the roof and dig their way through the ceiling until they have opened up an unconventional entrance to the room. We might wonder whether we would have gone to such lengths to bring a needy companion into Jesus' presence.

What I love most about this story, however, is contained in those two words 'let down.' They let their friend down. Being let down sounds more like a disappointment than a blessing. Yet whenever I read this story I remember that sometimes when life has 'let me down' this has been the fastest route to the feet of Jesus, who has then invited me to rise up again, healed and renewed, and continue the journey.

---

*When we feel let down, may we remember this story
and have the grace to look up, into the eyes of Jesus.*

MARGARET SILF

In truth and love:
2 and 3 John

In our present age the brevity of text messages reigns supreme; but at any other period of history the epistles of 2 and 3 John would have been considered to be brief in the extreme. The American theologian C. Clifton Black suggests these texts, at 245 words and 219 words respectively, are more like postcards than letters (The New Interpreter's Bible (NIB) Vol. XII, p. 448). He also describes 2 John as 'one of the usually neglected stepchildren in biblical interpretation'. In common with its companion letter, 3 John, it finds no place in the Revised Common Lectionary, and has thus received little or no attention from preachers and teachers. As a result, many congregations may be unaware that these two letters even exist!

These epistles are generally agreed to have been written by the same anonymous author (almost certainly along with 1 John). There are several common features. Both begin with 'The elder to… whom I love in [the] truth'. Both stress the vital importance of walking in the truth. Both express the author's wish to be able to visit the community soon, when he will be able to talk with them 'face to face'. And both write of the inadequacy of paper and ink to communicate as effectively as a personal encounter. The letters end with the sending of personal greetings, with 3 John adding that 'the friends there' should each be greeted by name.

Our sequence will begin with two pieces that will introduce the letters individually, in order to provide a foundation for the later reflections. For each of these, readers are encouraged to read through the entire letter and not just the opening verses quoted. For the remainder of the sequence we shall move backwards and forwards across both letters, focusing on particular themes and ideas as they occur. Some of the texts chosen will be very short. As we are dealing with pieces that together extend to only 28 verses, there will inevitably be a considerable amount of overlap and repetition in the texts chosen for each day's reflection. When repetition does occur, however, the aim will be to approach each recurrence from a different angle and perspective.

BARBARA MOSSE

In truth and love

The elder to the elect lady and her children, whom I love in the truth, and not only I but also all who know the truth, because of the truth that abides in us and will be with us for ever: Grace, mercy, and peace will be with us from God the Father and from Jesus Christ, the Father's Son, in truth and love.

In its length and expression, 2 John presents a letter form that was common in antiquity. Letters usually contained a request of some kind, and the conventional format comprised an opening greeting, the main body of the letter, which contained the request itself and how the letter's recipient would benefit from complying, and a gracious conclusion. The basic format is modified slightly here: its opening is more theologically developed than is usually the case, and following the request to follow the path of love and reject everything that would deceive, both benefits and warnings concerning compliance and non-compliance are expressed. The letter closes with greetings and an acknowledgement of the weakness of paper and ink to convey the author's true feelings when compared to the joy of a face-to-face encounter.

In writings of the New Testament period, 'elder' usually refers to someone who is to be treated with the respect and honour due to one's father (1 Timothy 5:1). Here, 'the elder' clearly has great affection for these people and feels a strong responsibility for their spiritual and moral welfare.

And who is the 'elect lady' to whom this letter is addressed? She may be a woman in whose home this particular church group is meeting, and her 'children' may be the individual members of that group. Or the term may be the author's coded reference to the church itself. Whoever these Christians are, the writer clearly feels a close kinship with them 'because of the truth that abides in us and will be with us for ever'.

Jesus said, 'If you continue in my word… you will know the truth, and the truth will make you free' (John 8:31–32). How may we discern 'the truth' within the complex network of patterns and relationships that make up our own lives?

BARBARA MOSSE

Walking in the truth

The elder to the beloved Gaius, whom I love in truth. Beloved, I pray that all may go well with you and that you may be in good health, just as it is well with your soul. I was overjoyed when some of the friends arrived and testified to your faithfulness to the truth, namely how you walk in the truth. I have no greater joy than this, to hear that my children are walking in the truth.

In this letter the author identifies himself again as 'the elder', but 3 John differs from its predecessor in being addressed to an individual – Gaius. As with the 'elect lady' of 2 John we have no way of knowing who precisely this person was, as Gaius was a very common name at this time. Acts 19:29 refers to a Gaius who was a Macedonian companion of Paul; in Romans 16:23 a Gaius is named as 'host to [Paul] and to the whole church'; and 1 Corinthians 1:14 names one Gaius as a Christian believer whom Paul baptised. We may not be able to identify Gaius precisely, but it is clear that both he and his correspondent relate warmly to one another in the fellowship of Christian love and truth, and share a concern for the healthy life and growth of the Christian community.

After the opening greeting, the elder moves briskly on to a question of hospitality (3 John 5–8), and closely follows this with a vexed question of local authority and leadership (3 John 9–11). Both of these important issues will be explored further in later reflections; we touch on them briefly here because both form vital components of what it means, for individuals and for the Christian community, to walk in the truth. It is to the concept of truth that this writer returns again and again, exploring what demands it makes of the believers in different practical situations. He weaves it through both letters like a golden thread.

The elder wrote, 'I have no greater joy than this, to hear that my children are walking in the truth' (3 John 4). In what ways can each of us seek to live in that truth today?

BARBARA MOSSE

Encouragement and warning

... let us love one another. And this is love, that we walk according to his commandments; this is the commandment just as you have heard it from the beginning – you must walk in it. Many deceivers have gone out into the world, those who do not confess that Jesus Christ has come in the flesh; any such person is the deceiver and the antichrist! Be on your guard, so that you do not lose what we have worked for, but may receive a full reward.

After a warm and encouraging opening, the elder's tone changes abruptly: 'Many deceivers have gone out into the world, those who do not confess that Jesus Christ has come in the flesh; any such person is the deceiver and the antichrist!' He may well have had in mind the 'false prophets' and 'ravenous wolves' about whom Jesus spoke so strongly (Matthew 7:15–23). Some critics have stumbled over the elder's words here, but this example from Matthew makes clear that this stance was, at times, a feature of Christ's teaching. We may find it difficult to hold these condemnatory words, re-emphasised in 2 John 10–11 (see tomorrow's text and reflection), alongside the Christian imperative to openness and hospitality. But in 2 John, balance is provided by the elder's opening injunction to 'love one another'.

This is easier said than done. You may, like me, have known churches where the fellowship was so ready to rush to judgement that any sense of real love was squashed out; but we only need to remember the horrible headlines around child abuse in the church to see what can happen when an out-of-control 'anything goes' mentality prevails. It isn't easy, but the life and teaching of Jesus provide us with both the foundation and the yardstick by which we can assess the integrity of our lives in him. By walking steadfastly and conscientiously in this love, we will be better able to discern any deviations from the pattern that Jesus has set.

In 1 John, the author urges his readers to 'test the spirits to see whether they are from God'. In the context of your church and your spiritual journey, how might you, both corporately and individually, 'test the spirits'?

BARBARA MOSSE

Hard judgement

Be on your guard, so that you do not lose what we have worked for, but may receive a full reward. Everyone who does not abide in the teaching of Christ, but goes beyond it, does not have God; whoever abides in the teaching has both the Father and the Son. Do not receive into the house or welcome anyone who comes to you and does not bring this teaching; for to welcome is to participate in the evil deeds of such a person.

Yesterday's reflection located the nub of the problem: it was absolutely critical for the early church that it hold firmly to the belief that Christ had actually come in the flesh. The belief that Jesus was both fully God and fully human is difficult enough to grasp today, in spite of the benefits of 2,000 years of hindsight. The early church struggled with the same dilemma. The heresies that sprang up in the early centuries appeared because people failed to hold on to this paradox. The Docetists believed that Christ's body was not physically real, while the followers of Arius believed Jesus was less than fully God. The elder's prime concern here is to draw some firm boundaries for the stability and integrity of the Christian community. While some appreciation of the historical context is vital to a constructive interpretation of this passage, its value to us lies in our reflection on our own attitudes to matters of faith and belief.

Perhaps we need to be content to see ourselves as a work in progress. Max Ehrmann's well-known poem 'Desiderata' encourages the believer, 'beyond a wholesome discipline, be gentle with yourself'. The truth of our belief in Christ is not proved through any successful experiment in the science laboratory. There are some things we will not be able fully to grasp this side of heaven, but, says the 14th-century anonymous author of *The Cloud of Unknowing*, 'love Jesus, and all he has is yours. Knit yourself to him by love and faith.'

How do you wrestle with this paradox? Are you able to acknowledge and then rise above the struggle, and simply love Jesus, knowing that all he has is yours?

BARBARA MOSSE

The call to hospitality

Beloved, you do faithfully whatever you do for the friends, even though they are strangers to you; they have testified to your love before the church. You will do well to send them on in a manner worthy of God; for they began their journey for the sake of Christ, accepting no support from non-believers. Therefore we ought to support such people, so that we may become co-workers with the truth.

The elder offers a sharp contrast between the community's need to reject those who preach false doctrine and the warm welcome that should be extended to the 'friends', 'even though they are strangers to you'. The elder here seems to be well aware of one of our basic human tendencies: the tendency to localism – being comfortable with our 'group' as it is, with the associated instinct to resist the change and disruption that will be inevitable if new people, and new challenges, are to be welcomed into the group.

It's one thing, perhaps, to recognise the clannish tendencies of some otherwise well-intentioned churches, but how do we feel about the same injunctions to hospitality when applied to our own homes? Many years ago, when I was a church worker in London, I opened the door to my home one day to a seemingly distressed young man who claimed that all his money had been stolen. I didn't give him money but invited him in and gave him some food. He then curled up on my sofa and – apparently – went to sleep. I was on my own, and still remember my anxiety at having to wake him up and ask him to leave, because I had to go to work.

There is a challenge for all of us, perhaps, in finding a balance between sensible caution – maybe 1 John's instruction to 'test the spirits' is important here – and Jesus' teaching about welcome and hospitality: 'Whoever welcomes this child in my name welcomes me, and whoever welcomes me welcomes the one who sent me' (Luke 9:48).

In what ways do you allow yourself to be challenged by the needs of hospitality, both in your own home and within your church fellowship?

BARBARA MOSSE

Disputed authority

I have written something to the church; but Diotrephes, who likes to put himself first, does not acknowledge our authority. So if I come, I will call attention to what he is doing in spreading false charges against us. And not content with those charges, he refuses to welcome the friends, and even prevents those who want to do so and expels them from the church. Beloved, do not imitate what is evil but imitate what is good. Whoever does good is from God; whoever does evil has not seen God.

We have no idea who Diotrephes was or how he came to wield such power in this community. The elder considers his influence to be malign for a number of reasons. Diotrephes, says the elder, 'likes to put himself first' and 'does not acknowledge our authority'. He is spreading doubt among the community by promoting false charges against the elder. The elder complains that Diotrephes' mischief-making is striking at the very heart of the community's life. He is refusing to welcome friends who are seeking the community's hospitality, and actively prevents those who wish to offer a welcome from doing so, expelling them from the community. It is interesting, in the context of the doctrinal concerns expressed in 2 John, that none of the elder's complaints here are concerned with matters of correct or incorrect belief!

There is much here about the nature and exercise of power, and elements of what we read here may strike chords within our own experience of church life. Wherever or however we may encounter such aggrandisement, such behaviour strikes at the root of Jesus' teaching: 'You know that among the Gentiles… their rulers lord it over them. But it is not so among you; but whoever wishes to become great among you must be your servant, and whoever wishes to be first among you must be slave of all' (Mark 10: 42–44).

Reflect for a few moments on the use and abuse of power in the church, and in our world today. How does what you see compare with Jesus' modelling of a very different kind of leadership – that of a servant? Can you identify any, in the church or the world, who are leading effectively following the pattern of Christ?

BARBARA MOSSE

Love one another

… let us love one another. And this is love, that we walk according to his commandments; this is the commandment just as you have heard it from the beginning – you must walk in it.

The elder assures the 'dear lady' that he is not writing a new commandment, 'but one we have had from the beginning'. This recalls Jesus' teaching to his disciples: 'I give you a new commandment, that you love one another. Just as I have loved you, you also should love one another' (John 13:34).

How can we begin to obey this commandment? We can take a long, honest look at some of our behaviour and attitudes, and resolve to behave better in future. But deep down we know our weakness; we know the situations that provoke our envy, resentment, over-the-top anger or whatever. We are human and know that, despite our best intentions, we will fail again.

The 16th-century Spanish mystic St John of the Cross suggests a complementary approach. This is the way of inner silence, where we come before God not primarily to bombard him with our needs and concerns but to listen to him within the depths of our heart. In those depths God shines with what John of the Cross calls 'a very loving light'. Our difficulty lies in the hidden grime that loving light reveals; our instinct is to shy away and pretend it's not there. But if we have the courage to stay with what God is showing us, he will gradually work away at our problem areas and our lives, and our loving will be progressively transformed.

Sit in your prayer space, and light a candle if you find that helpful. Take a few moments to relax your body and your breathing. Allow your mind to rest on a simple prayer word, such as 'God', 'Jesus' or 'Love'. Your mind will be fretful because of your lack of activity, but don't worry; this is normal. Simply bring your mind back, gently and without self-condemnation, to your prayer word. However distracted you feel, God is at work in the deepest part of your being. Believe that he is at work, even if you feel nothing is happening.

BARBARA MOSSE

God the Father

Whoever does good is from God; whoever does evil has not seen God.

Over the next three days we shall be considering what these two brief epistles have to say about God as Father, Son and Holy Spirit. References to God the Father in 2 John and 3 John are few, and refer only indirectly to the nature of God the Father. It is by looking at the behaviour of other people that we learn something of what God is or is not like. When the elder urges Gaius to practise hospitality and care for others, he encourages them to 'do faithfully whatever you do for the friends, even though they are strangers to you… You will do well to send them on in a manner worthy of God' (3 John 5–6). Our given text deduces the total goodness of God from the behaviour of human beings: those who do good reflect God's goodness; those who do evil have never seen him and do not know him.

Have you come across people who clearly reflect the goodness of God? We may all be familiar with St Francis of Assisi, or more recently Mother Teresa of Calcutta. But for many of us there may be others who are closer to home, people whose lives radiate a goodness that mysteriously seems to come from within. And such people may – or may not! – carry the 'Christian' label. For such a quality to be sincere, the person showing it needs to be unconscious of their 'goodness'. Even Jesus wouldn't accept it when an anxious young man addressed him as 'Good Teacher', replying sharply, 'Why do you call me good? No one is good but God alone' (Mark 10:18).

How do we reflect the goodness of God in our own lives? This is a difficult question, because the moment we become conscious of our own goodness – or lack of it – we take our eyes off God and focus back on ourselves. The danger here is that we will stoke up our pride and pamper our ego. The work is God's, not ours, and our task is to cooperate with what our heavenly Father is doing.

Continue with your silent practice of yesterday, inviting God to reveal further insights in the beam of his 'very loving light'.

BARBARA MOSSE

God the Son

Many deceivers have gone out into the world, those who do not confess that Jesus Christ has come in the flesh... Everyone who does not abide in the teaching of Christ, but goes beyond it, does not have God; whoever abides in the teaching has both Father and Son.

Two vitally important points concerning Jesus are expressed in today's passage. We have already touched on the first (Wednesday 11 July), which focused on the importance of the belief that Christ had actually come in the flesh and was not some embodied spirit only masquerading as a human being. But some further ideas are added here. The elder writes approvingly of those who 'abide' in the teaching of Christ (this is also the primary image used in 1 John to describe the believer's relationship with Christ), while rejecting those who 'go beyond' Christ's teaching, without authority or restraint. The elder doesn't specify what this 'going beyond' might look like, but most commentators assume that it is related to his insistence that Christ is both human and divine, not one or the other.

The second point is highlighted by the statement that 'whoever abides in the teaching has both Father and Son'. The union of the Father and the Son is an idea repeatedly stressed in John's Gospel, and it is a teaching that Jesus' disciples found particularly difficult to grasp. 'Lord, show us the Father,' said Philip, 'and we will be satisfied' (John 14:8). And we can sense the exasperation in Jesus' reply: 'Have I been with you all this time, Philip, and you still do not know me? Whoever has seen me has seen the Father' (John 14:9). Would our question to Jesus be the same as Philip's? As we reflect today on the profound truth of the union of Father and Son, we may like to consider Jesus' reply to Philip, substituting our own name for his.

'Have I been with you all this time, _____, and you still do not know me? Whoever has seen me has seen the Father... Do you not believe that I am in the Father and the Father is in me?' (John 14:9–10).

BARBARA MOSSE

God the Holy Spirit

I was overjoyed to find some of your children walking in the truth, just as we have been commanded by the Father... I was overjoyed when some of the friends arrived and testified to your faithfulness to the truth, namely, how you walk in the truth. I have no greater joy than this, to hear that my children are walking in the truth.

It may seem slightly strange to be considering what 2 and 3 John have to say about the Holy Spirit, when neither letter actually mentions the Spirit directly. As we have already seen, however, one theme that occurs repeatedly in both epistles is the importance of 'truth'. It is truth that holds together the love that exists between the elder and those with whom he corresponds; it is truth in which the followers of Jesus walk, and the believers are promised that same truth will abide in them for ever. There is no direct naming of the Spirit here, but when we consider other writings in the Johannine corpus we see that the truth's link with the Holy Spirit is made very clear. In 1 John (thought to be by the same author), the connection is made explicit: 'And the Spirit is the one that testifies, for the Spirit is the truth' (1 John 5:6). And in John's Gospel, Jesus tells his disciples that 'when the Spirit of truth comes, he will guide you into all the truth' (John 16:13).

This truth is not always easy for us to hear and accept. I am reminded of an image from the Bayeux Tapestry, where someone is pictured urging his troops into battle with a staff. The accompanying caption states that he is 'comforting' the troops. The Authorised Version of the Bible speaks of the Holy Spirit as 'the Comforter', but as with the Bayeux Tapestry image, the comfort offered by the Holy Spirit is more likely to take the form of a bracing confrontation with God's truth rather than physical ease or freedom from pain or discomfort.

---

*'And I will ask the Father, and he will give you another Advocate,
to be with you for ever. This is the Spirit of Truth, whom the world cannot
receive, because it neither sees him nor knows him' (John 14:16–17).
How do we experience the 'comfort' of the Holy Spirit in our own lives?*

BARBARA MOSSE

What we have seen and heard

But now, dear lady, I ask you, not as though I were writing you a new commandment… let us love one another. And this is love, that we walk according to his commandments; this is the commandment just as you have heard it from the beginning – you must walk in it.

All the way back through Israel's history, we see how important it is that the people regularly remember and re-enact those significant events in their past that have established or redefined the nation's relationship with God. There are many such examples, but probably the most significant is recorded in Exodus 12:1–20. Before the nation's departure from Egypt, God gives Moses and Aaron precise instructions for the meal that would be later celebrated as the Passover, and urges on them the duty and importance of national memory: 'This day shall be a day of remembrance for you. You shall celebrate it as a festival to the Lord; throughout your generations you shall observe it as a perpetual ordinance' (Exodus 12:14).

From the days of the early church to the present, Christians have continued to remember. Each week the church faithfully follows the instructions of Jesus, who when celebrating the last supper told his disciples that the bread and the wine were his body and his blood and commanded them to 'do this in remembrance of me' (Luke 22:19).

It may have been C.S. Lewis who, when asked why he went to church, replied that he went in order to remind himself of who – and whose – he was. The elder urges the people to remember the commandment 'we have had from the beginning'. The pace of life today is frantic and many of us lead stressful and fractured lives. We can all benefit from personal acts of remembrance, whether privately or within the communal worship of our local church. Such acts have the potential to anchor us more deeply in God, and to re-order our priorities in the light of his love.

Remember the days of old, the years long past; ask your father, and he will inform you; your elders, and they will tell you (Deuteronomy 32:7). What part does 'remembering' play in your faith journey?

BARBARA MOSSE

Anticipating Christ's return

Many deceivers have gone out into the world, those who do not confess that Jesus Christ has come in the flesh; any such person is the deceiver and the antichrist! Be on your guard, so that you do not lose what we have worked for, but may receive a full reward.

It is in these two verses that 2 John finds its greatest resonance with John's first epistle. Both letters are concerned with the threat posed by deceivers who do not believe that Jesus Christ has come in the flesh, as opposed to those who do. The term 'antichrist' belongs to a genre of literature known as apocalyptic – concerned with the end times. These disciples believed that Christ would soon return, and the elder urges them to 'be on your guard'.

How does this teaching affect us today? We will all be familiar with some of the embarrassing announcements that crop up from time to time from people who declare that the world will come to an end on a specific date. The said date passes without incident, and after a time of re-grouping another date is announced. Clearly, this is not what scripture is asking us to do, as Jesus makes clear in the Gospels (Matthew 25:13).

The elder approaches the community of 2 John with what might be called binocular vision: his concern is twofold. Directly in front of him is the immediate worry: how to prevent the community from being torn apart by schism, in the way the community of 1 John seems to have been. But behind the immediate concern lies the need to be prepared and ready for Christ's return, whether that return was imminent or to be delayed.

As we know, the delay continues. How do we, 2,000 years on from these events, respond to the continuing imperative to 'keep awake' on our own spiritual journeys?

'Keep awake therefore, for you know neither the day nor the hour'
(Matthew 25:13). How does your church approach this teaching?
How do we maintain a state of watchfulness and readiness, while
at the same time giving due consideration to the daily demands of
the world in which we all live?

BARBARA MOSSE

The yardstick of goodness

Beloved, do not imitate what is evil but imitate what is good. Whoever does good is from God; whoever does evil has not seen God.

We first reflected on the second part of this text when we were considering what the epistle had to say about God the Father. We return to it now, this time focusing on the sentence which precedes it: 'Beloved, do not imitate what is evil, but imitate what is good.' The use of the term 'imitate' here is interesting, because it is found nowhere else in the Johannine corpus. Although Jesus did not use the term, he did nevertheless urge his disciples to follow him. Several of these instances suggest his hearers are being encouraged to model their lives on Christ's way of being, rather than simply to accompany him on his travels (Luke 9:23; 14:27). And there is a liberal sprinkling of references among other New Testament writings. Paul urges the members of the Corinthian church to 'be imitators of me, as I am of Christ' (1 Corinthians 11:1). The Thessalonians are encouraged in a similar manner (1 Thessalonians 1:6). And the Ephesians are urged to 'be imitators of God, as beloved children, and live in love, as Christ loved us' (Ephesians 5:1).

The ideal of the imitation of Christ has been a key element in Christianity since the earliest times. In his book *The Imitation of Christ*, the 15th-century scholar Thomas à Kempis claimed that the life and way of Christ should be the first priority 'if we desire true enlightenment and freedom from all blindness of heart'. He also stated that a simple heart-response to God was more important than understanding abstruse academic theology: 'Lofty words do not make a man just or holy; but a good life makes him dear to God.' There is no one blueprint for this 'imitation'.

Many today are encouraged to 'imitate' their heroes through their (over-) promotion through the media. But Jesus is a real person, not an advertiser's gimmick. His way leads to life, not death. How may we imitate him today?

BARBARA MOSSE

Who is Jesus?

Grace, mercy, and peace will be with us from God the Father and from Jesus Christ, the Father's Son, in truth and love.

We conclude our series of reflections on 2 and 3 John by pondering a question that has puzzled and teased the human race throughout the history of the Christian church: who, precisely, is Jesus? 2 John firmly claims that Jesus was truly man and truly the Son of God, and both epistles stress that a life with Jesus is one characterised by love and truth. Elsewhere in the New Testament King Herod's associates thought Jesus was John the Baptist raised from the dead (Mark 6:14). When Jesus asked his disciples who the people thought he was, they answered, 'John the Baptist; and others, Elijah; and still others, one of the prophets' (Mark 8:28). Jesus pushed the question further, asking his disciples what they thought, and Peter answers with a flash of divine insight: 'You are the Messiah' (Mark 6:29).

Before Jesus' crucifixion, the high priest also wants to know: 'Are you the Messiah, the Son of the Blessed One?' Luke and Matthew report an enigmatic response from Jesus, but in Mark's Gospel his reply is more direct: 'I am; and "you will see the Son of Man seated at the right hand of the Power, and coming with the clouds of heaven"' (Mark 14:61–62).

The questions continue to this day. Many people believe Jesus to be a good man and an outstanding teacher, but stop short of accepting his divine nature. Christians believe Jesus is the Son of God as a matter of faith, not scientific fact. Perhaps, when all has been said and done, Simon Peter speaks for us all: 'Lord, to whom can we go? You have the words of eternal life. We have come to believe and know that you are the Holy One of God' (John 6:68–69).

It is in the Gospels that we see most clearly who Jesus is, in word and action. Consider reading one of the Gospels through, slowly and reflectively, a few verses or a chapter at a time.

BARBARA MOSSE

My favourite prayers

To be absolutely honest, I think my favourite prayers are the ones I have almost 'in conversation', when I am stepping out along a pilgrimage road, my pack on my back, with nothing to do but walk for many hours before sunset brings an evening meal and a well-earned rest. The prayers I say cover a wide range – intercessions for people I have met along the road or left behind at home, prayers of thanksgiving for the glorious creation that surrounds me, and occasional, precious prayers of faithful acceptance of God's will for me, whatever that might entail. These, I think, are my prayers of growth, discovery and deepening relationship, but they cannot be written down or even shared by anyone other than a pilgrim and her God. However, one cannot spend 18 years as a Church of England priest without some of what are the most beautiful, heartfelt words ever written sinking deep into one's soul, becoming part of the essence of one's humanity. It is these that I offer to you over the next seven days.

Looking back over the prayers I have chosen, they seem to cover a wide range of approaches and experiences. Some, such as the one by Anselm, capture the challenge of faith, the great task of having 'assurance of things hoped for, the conviction of things not seen' (Hebrews 11:1). Others are prayers for activists who fear they may stray far from God's way inadvertently – how typical of busy people that, immediately after his prayer at the Battle of Edgehill, Jacob Astley's next words were 'March on, boys!' The simple, ancient rhythms of Evening Prayer from the Book of Common Prayer were part of my childhood and remain a precious feature of my ministry today. To utter prayers for a safe ending in a small country church whose east window looks out on to quiet hills brings to mind those countless generations who have uttered the same words in the same place, linking the congregation with the company of saints who share our prayers as they gather before the throne of grace. They have found their 'safe lodging' and 'holy rest'; we must be confident that we will too.

SALLY WELCH

'A quick understanding'

And there shall come forth a rod out of the stem of Jesse, and a Branch shall grow out of his roots: And the spirit of the Lord shall rest upon him, the spirit of wisdom and understanding, the spirit of counsel and might, the spirit of knowledge and of the fear of the Lord; And shall make him of quick understanding in the fear of the Lord: and he shall not judge after the sight of his eyes, neither reprove after the hearing of his ears: But with righteousness shall he judge the poor, and reprove with equity for the meek of the earth… And righteousness shall be the girdle of his loins, and faithfulness the girdle of his reins.

'His delight shall be in the fear of the Lord.' It seems rather a leap from the 'quick understanding in the fear of the Lord' of the Authorised Version to the 'delight in the fear of the Lord' of modern translations, but closer exploration of the text reveals that this change is a natural progression of understanding. The focus here is on the Hebrew word *ruach*, which has a range of meanings – spirit, breath, wind, smell. Fragrant substance can be breathed in, smells reaching the brain in a quicker, more direct way than sight or sound. Smell is the last sense to fade and, as we know, it can provoke profound reactions when linked with thoughts or memories.

Isaiah tells us that the Spirit will give us an understanding of the things that concern the worship of God. This understanding will be both immediate and all-embracing, filling our souls and bodies, refreshing and delighting us in much the same way that the scent of fresh bread or newly mown grass can give us joy and wonder at being alive. Rossetti's prayer is that we may keep this sense of immediate connection with God throughout the day and that we may thereby become sensitive to his direction in a new and complete way.

Make us of quick understanding and tender conscience, O Lord;
that understanding we may obey every word of yours this day and
discerning may follow every suggestion of your indwelling Spirit. Speak
Lord, for your servant is listening through Jesus Christ our Lord.
(Christina Rossetti, 1830–94)

SALLY WELCH

Busy, busy, busy

Then [Ruth] fell prostrate, with her face to the ground, and said to him, 'Why have I found favour in your sight, that you should take notice of me, when I am a foreigner?' But Boaz answered her, 'All that you have done for your mother-in-law since the death of your husband has been fully told me, and how you left your father and mother and your native land and came to a people that you did not know before. May the Lord reward you for your deeds, and may you have a full reward from the Lord, the God of Israel, under whose wings you have come for refuge!'

Boaz's generosity to Ruth, a poor widow, marks the beginning of a new chapter for both Ruth and Boaz, one which ends with the continuation of the house of David, stretching forward to the birth of Christ himself. But Boaz would not have had a part to play at all if he had not conducted his everyday working life in a way that honoured God. Ruth is allowed to glean the crops left behind by the harvesters in the way that the Jewish laws instructed, but was often not followed by the Jewish people. More than that, however, Boaz has heard of her gracious behaviour in accompanying her widowed mother-in-law to her home country. Boaz notes this and approves of it; he allows this to be reflected in his attitude towards her and she is invited by him to share the labourers' meal. 'May the Lord reward you for your deeds' says Boaz to Ruth, and God indeed rewards them both.

The prayer of Jacob Astley, made just before the Battle of Edgehill in 1642, echoes this awareness that a relationship with God should not begin and end with Sunday worship but overflow to every aspect of our lives. It also acknowledges our human weakness in so often neglecting to do this, and asks God's forgiveness if, caught up in the activity of the moment, we fail to listen for his voice.

O Lord, thou knowest how busy I must be this day.
If I forget thee, do not forget me.
(Jacob Astley, 1st Baron Astley of Reading)

SALLY WELCH

Seeking God

O God, you are my God, I seek you, my soul thirsts for you; my flesh faints for you, as in a dry and weary land where there is no water. So I have looked upon you in the sanctuary, beholding your power and glory. Because your steadfast love is better than life, my lips will praise you. So I will bless you as long as I live; I will lift up my hands and call on your name. My soul is satisfied as with a rich feast, and my mouth praises you with joyful lips when I think of you on my bed, and meditate on you in the watches of the night; for you have been my help, and in the shadow of your wings I sing for joy. My soul clings to you; your right hand upholds me.

How beautifully Anselm captures the mystery that lies at the heart of our faith! A 12th-century theologian and philosopher, Anselm describes our often painful searching after God, longing to meet him in a desperate way 'as in a dry and weary land where there is no water', aware that our very life depends upon finding God. Yet despite the fact that we are created by God, we do not know him; we give him our lives but he is unseen by us. Anselm's prayer answers our own as he reminds himself and us that it is in the very act of seeking God that we will find him.

O my God teach my heart where and how to seek you,
where and how to find you…
You are my God and you are my All and I have never seen you.
You have made me and remade me, you have bestowed on me
all the good things I possess,
Still I do not know you…
I have not yet done that for which I was made….
Teach me to seek you…
I cannot seek you unless you teach me or find you
unless you show yourself to me.
Let me seek you in my desire, let me desire you in my seeking.
Let me find you by loving you, let me love you when I find you.
(St Anselm of Canterbury)

SALLY WELCH

God of our pilgrimage

In days to come the mountain of the Lord's house shall be established as the highest of the mountains, and shall be raised above the hills; all the nations shall stream to it. Many peoples shall come and say, 'Come, let us go up to the mountain of the Lord, to the house of the God of Jacob; that he may teach us his ways and that we may walk in his paths.' For out of Zion shall go forth instruction, and the word of the Lord from Jerusalem. He shall judge between the nations, and shall arbitrate for many peoples; they shall beat their swords into ploughshares, and their spears into pruning hooks; nation shall not lift up sword against nation, neither shall they learn war any more.

A recent news article noted that an increase in mountain rescues was the result of unprepared hikers relying on Google Maps and satnavs, which would then fail. A knowledge of map-reading and compass use, readers were told, is essential when climbing mountains. So too we must ensure that we follow a reliable guide on our path through life.

In this complicated world, fraught with challenges and conflict, the vision of Isaiah stands as a glorious promise. But we will never attain this goal unless we journey towards it. We must make our pilgrimage to the 'mountain of the Lord', because it is only when we reach the 'house of the God of Jacob' that we will be able to learn his ways and walk in his paths.

So we pray, with the whole people of God, for the strength and grace to follow the true path, not lured away by the siren calls of materialistic, confrontational living, but directing our steps towards the gate of mercy, following in trust the one who leads us.

The almighty and everlasting God, who is the way, the truth, and the life, dispose your journey according to his good pleasure, send his angel Raphael to keep you in this your pilgrimage, and both conduct you in peace on your way to the place where you would be, and bring you back again on your return to us in safety. (Sarum Missal*, 13th century)

---

*The Sarum Rite was the liturgical form used in most of the English church prior to the introduction of the first Book of Common Prayer in 1549.

SALLY WELCH

A constant support

Do not let your hearts be troubled. Believe in God, believe also in me. In my Father's house there are many dwelling places. If it were not so, would I have told you that I go to prepare a place for you? And if I go and prepare a place for you, I will come again and will take you to myself, so that where I am, there you may be also. And you know the way to the place where I am going.' Thomas said to him, 'Lord, we do not know where you are going. How can we know the way?' Jesus said to him, 'I am the way, and the truth, and the life. No one comes to the Father except through me. If you know me, you will know my Father also. From now on you do know him and have seen him.'

Whenever I read this passage, the countless faces of mourners whose loved ones we have gathered to bury float across my mind's eye. Shocked, angry, tear-soaked faces distorted with sadness, their eyes fixed on me, hoping I can help them to make sense of the tragedy that has blighted their lives.

I can't, of course, but I can tell them of one who can, who holds their suffering in his hands, who walks beside them in the valley over which death has cast his long, cold shadow. I can speak of Christ's love for each one of them and for his promise that in their journey he has gone ahead of us to prepare a 'safe lodging' for each of us. I can join with them in asking for God's love to support us now and 'all day long', until we can join him and those we love but see no longer in our Father's house.

Support us, O Lord,
all the day long of this troublous life,
until the shadows lengthen and the evening comes,
the busy world is hushed,
the fever of life is over
and our work is done.
Then, Lord, in your mercy grant us a safe lodging,
a holy rest, and peace at the last;
through Christ our Lord.
(Book of Common Prayer 1928)

SALLY WELCH

Watch, O Lord

Guided by the Spirit, Simeon came into the temple; and when the parents brought in the child Jesus, to do for him what was customary under the law, Simeon took him in his arms and praised God, saying, 'Master, now you are dismissing your servant in peace, according to your word; for my eyes have seen your salvation, which you have prepared in the presence of all peoples, a light for revelation to the Gentiles and for glory to your people Israel.'

I am a habitual worrier. If there is a problem that can be foreseen, I will anticipate it. If an event can have a number of possible outcomes, I will imagine all of them and be anxious about every single one. Time and again I consciously try to commit my worries and burdens to God, picturing myself laying them at the foot of the cross, kneeling in acknowledgement that Jesus is Lord and that I can have complete faith in him. In my imagination, I turn and walk away, only, moments later, to scurry back, take up my figurative burdens and pick over them once more, anxiously tugging at the threads of hope and faith that I have bound them in, until they come loose and run around my mind once more.

This prayer of Augustine then becomes a rock upon which I can lean, giving charge to Christ over all those for whom I have care, allowing them to be taken from me by 'angels and saints' so much more skilled than I in love and tenderness, enabling me and them to rest in God's peace. Freed from my burdens I can lift my hands in praise with Simeon and countless others, glorifying God and witnessing to the light of his love.

Watch, O Lord, with those who wake, or watch, or weep tonight, and give your angels and saints charge over those who sleep. Tend your sick ones, O Lord Christ, rest your weary ones, bless your dying ones, soothe your suffering ones, pity your afflicted ones, shield your joyous ones. And all for your love's sake. Amen
(St Augustine of Hippo)

SALLY WELCH

A bright flame

They set out from Succoth, and camped at Etham, on the edge of the wilderness. The Lord went in front of them in a pillar of cloud by day, to lead them along the way, and in a pillar of fire by night, to give them light, so that they might travel by day and by night. Neither the pillar of cloud by day nor the pillar of fire by night left its place in front of the people.

The children of Israel have been led out into the desert, that vast, formless wilderness that will become the crucible for their transformation. They enter the desert as children, content to be led by others, seeing only their own acts and deeds as having any significance, happy in the temporary satisfaction of immediate needs. The space is a liminal one, a threshold, where identities become fluid so that they can be reformed and changed. It is a harsh landscape containing only the bare minimum necessary for survival. Within this place they will be tried and tested as individuals and as people. They will fail many times and be punished, but learning is in the failure and the pain and gradually the children of God become God's people. A new awareness of their relationship with God develops, a readiness to take responsibility for themselves, a desire to grow into their full potential as human beings. And all the while they are accompanied by God, who guides them with fire by night and cloud by day, along the path that leads to the promised land.

We cannot see the flame or the star, but we can discern their guidance. The path may not be an actual physical one, but it is clearly marked out for those who seek it. We must pray for the gifts of discernment, the grace to listen. Then we must place our trust in the shepherd, who will lead us home.

Be, Lord Jesus, a bright flame before me,
a guiding star above me,
a smooth path below me,
a kindly shepherd behind me:
today, tonight, and forever.
(St Columba)

SALLY WELCH

Unsung heroes of the Old Testament

If, like me, you attended Sunday school in your younger years, you will probably have heard of the exciting exploits of Moses, David, Daniel and other Old Testament heroes from your teachers. But there is another, lesser-known, group of people to be found in the earlier books of the Bible who are heroes nonetheless and also well worth our attention. Over the next fortnight we will be taking a look at some of the people who make only brief appearances in the Old Testament, men and women who, despite their short time on the stage of unfolding biblical revelation, have left us something of value and in one or two cases have affected the course of history.

Some of their names may be familiar: Deborah and Reuben, for example. Others, like Ebed-melech and Jabez, may be less so. But no doubt a good preacher could produce a full sermon from each. We have only a few paragraphs available for each of these bit-part players in the biblical drama, but as we take that brief look at them let us dwell on the contribution that each one made in their own day, and see if there is some aspect that we can both learn from and apply to our own life and situation.

However, a word of caution! I have enjoyed the meditations in *New Daylight* for many years. For me, their value lies to a great extent in the variety of approaches and insights that the various contributors bring to each daily reading. As I read, I sometimes find myself saying, 'I wonder why they didn't say something like… in their comments?' I am sure many of you too will want to add your own thoughts to some of these notes. If so, then they will have achieved their purpose.

You may even disagree with what I write! If my great namesake St Paul could read your thoughts, I'm sure he would shout a loud 'Hallelujah!' because that was the way he liked to teach – by saying something a bit outside the square in the hope of provoking a response.

PAUL GRAVELLE

Reuben: merciful but weak!

'Here comes that dreamer!' they said to each other, 'Come now, let's kill him and throw him into one of these cisterns and say that a ferocious animal devoured him. Then we'll see what comes of his dreams.' When Reuben heard this, he tried to rescue [Joseph] from their hands. 'Let's not take his life,' he said. 'Don't shed any blood. Throw him into this cistern here in the wilderness, but don't lay a hand on him.' Reuben said this to rescue him from them and take him back to his father.

Reuben was Jacob's eldest son and clearly felt his responsibility keenly, even though he lacked the authority among his brothers to prevent them from selling Joseph into slavery. On his return to the cistern later, now empty of young Joseph, verse 29 relates that Reuben tore his clothes (a traditional sign of great anguish) and cried, 'Where can I turn now?'

However, Reuben's apparent failure in this turned out to be one of the turning points in history. Joseph, as we know, became the virtual ruler in Egypt, and what followed – the oppression of his descendants, the exodus, the establishment of the nation of Israel and eventually the events of the Gospels themselves – has brought us to where we are today.

Reuben could easily be overlooked as a weak man, a failure. Yet God used his very ineffectiveness to bring about amazing things; and we, along with all the Christians down through the centuries, are the fortunate beneficiaries.

What about our failures? We have all experienced times when we know we could have done much better. Are we just to 'do a Reuben' – do the equivalent of tearing our clothes and say, 'What on earth can I do now?' Time and again through history God has shown a unique ability for bringing good out of even the most terrible evil. He is an unchanging God. He can still bring success out of even our worst failures. Sometimes, says James 4:2, we do not receive because we do not ask!

Lord, I know you are always ready to forgive my failures. I thank you for the wonderful good you brought about from Reuben's weakness. Please bring some good result when my weakness causes me to fail. Amen

PAUL GRAVELLE

Miriam: sister of Moses

Miriam and Aaron began to talk against Moses… 'Has the Lord spoken only through Moses?' they asked. 'Hasn't he also spoken through us?' And the Lord heard this… He said, 'Listen to my words: When there is a prophet among you, I, the Lord, reveal myself to them in visions, I speak to them in dreams. But this is not true of my servant Moses… With him I speak face to face…' The anger of the Lord burned against them, and he left them. When the cloud lifted from above the tent, Miriam's skin was leprous – it became as white as snow…

We first meet a much younger Miriam, putting herself at considerable risk by watching over her baby brother, floating in his basket among the reeds at the edge of the Nile. Sadly this selfless action is overshadowed by the incident we have just read, in which her jealousy creeps in to paint a much unhappier picture.

Did God see Miriam as the ringleader in this family spat, and Aaron as the weaker accessory? God certainly took the sin of jealousy seriously and Miriam received a just punishment. Aaron, however, pleads for help and the story concludes with Moses interceding for the pair.

Jealousy is always there, waiting to pop up to the surface like the gas in the mud pools we are so familiar with here in New Zealand. But, unlike the mud pools, we can keep it to ourselves and not let it out into the open. The problem was that Miriam began to talk about it.

It happens in churches; it happens in families. If you're anything like me, you experience a little frisson of envy whenever you hear of someone's good fortune. That's natural enough; but when the 'If only…' turns to 'Why him?' or 'Why her?' we are sliding into jealousy and are urgently in need of God's forgiveness.

If your church offers the rite of confession in any form, I urge you not to treat it lightly but to make the most of it. The words 'God forgives you, be at peace' are wonderful words to hear.

Lord, when there is division among families all around me
(and even in my own family), make me a channel of your peace.

PAUL GRAVELLE

Caleb: man of vision

At the end of forty days they returned from exploring the land. They came back to Moses and Aaron and… reported to them… 'We went into the land to which you sent us, and it does flow with milk and honey!… But the people who live there are powerful, and the cities are fortified and very large…' Then Caleb silenced the people before Moses and said, 'We should go up and take possession of the land, for we can certainly do it.' But the men who had gone with him… spread among the Israelites a bad report about the land they had explored.

The Israelite people were easily discouraged. Rather than follow Caleb's strategy, they decided it would be better to go back to Egypt! It is worth reading all about this in the next chapter when you have time. The result was a 40-year period of wandering in the desert, during which the majority of them died, never to see the promised land.

What was it about Caleb that made him so confident of victory if the people would only press onward? God's subsequent word to Moses provides the answer: 'because my servant Caleb has a different spirit and follows me wholeheartedly, I will bring him into the land he went to, and his descendants will inherit it' (Numbers 14:24). Caleb and the new leader, Joshua, were indeed the sole surviving adults to cross the Jordan years later.

Could we infer then that having a 'different spirit' is a hallmark of those who can see unerringly the way that God wants his people to go in any given circumstance? We can certainly say that the Holy Spirit is given to Christians to guide their own footsteps, and indeed to enable them in helping others in their walk through life. There is no doubt too that half-heartedness in our relationship with God is no way to anticipate the kind of revelatory vision that was accorded to Caleb. It is only by following God wholeheartedly through his Son that we can hope to 'have the mind of Christ' (1 Corinthians 2:16). That is exactly what the Spirit is able to do for us!

Holy Spirit, work in us so that we may indeed have the mind of Christ and receive from you the direction we need to follow you wholeheartedly.

PAUL GRAVELLE

Deborah: prophetic leader

Now Deborah, a prophet, the wife of Lappidoth, was leading Israel at that time. She held court under the Palm of Deborah... and the Israelites went up to her to have their disputes decided. She sent for Barak... and said to him, 'The Lord, the God of Israel, commands you: "Go, take with you ten thousand men... and lead them up to Mount Tabor. I will lure Sisera, the commander of Jabin's army, with his chariots and his troops to the Kishon River and give him into your hands."'

The Israelites were being tyrannised by the Canaanite king Jabin. The story in Judges 4 and 5 is really more about Sisera and Jael – the woman who kills Sisera – than about Deborah herself, but Deborah is still remarkable for being a respected female leader in a male-dominated age and for exercising her prophetic gift in a manner that was to mark out Jael as one of Israel's great heroines.

In the Old Testament, prophecy is a gift attributed only to designated prophets and occasionally kings; it is not a gift available to just anyone. After Pentecost, prophecy took on a completely new characteristic. An example of this occurred in Ephesus when Paul, on one of his missionary journeys, discovered some followers of John the Baptist who had never heard about the Holy Spirit. He 'placed his hands on them, the Holy Spirit came on them, and they spoke in tongues and prophesied' (Acts 19:6). These were not people in any kind of leadership.

It is a great gift to the church – and a blessing to the world at large – when leaders in the church exercise a truly prophetic ministry. But prophecy is no longer the exclusive role of leaders, and the church needs all of its members to speak out the Lord's message in a prophetic way. Paul, in writing to the Corinthian church about spiritual gifts, says, 'I would like every one of you to speak in tongues, but I would rather have you prophesy' (1 Corinthians 14:5). What applied to the church then is just as applicable for us today.

Lord, help me to recognise your words when you give them to me and give me the opportunity and the courage to speak them out. Amen

PAUL GRAVELLE

Jabez: honoured man of prayer

Now Jabez was more honourable than his brothers... And Jabez called on the God of Israel saying, 'Oh, that you would bless me indeed, and enlarge my territory, that your hand would be with me, and that you would keep me from evil, that I may not cause pain!' So God granted him what he requested.

Bruce Wilkinson's little book *The Prayer of Jabez* has led many thousands of Christians to use this prayer in their daily devotions over recent years. This is strange because Jabez's prayer at first glance seems to be selfish, and some commentators have been critical of it for that reason.

It is important, however, that we ask God to bless us and to 'enlarge our territory', recognising that this is a way of asking God to give us greater opportunities to serve him. It is also helpful to invoke the hand of God to keep us from evil, both physical and spiritual, as we do so.

One of the reasons why so many Christians are using Jabez's prayer is that God granted his requests. Not only was Jabez a man of honourable reputation; he had asked God for the right things in his context. If we are serious in asking God to give us fresh opportunities of service, it is surely right to expect that he will grant our requests to that end.

I have been concluding my own personal prayers with the prayer of Jabez for many years now and can testify that God has blessed me indeed. I'm not talking about financial blessings, although my pension in retirement is sufficient for my needs, but God has certainly increased the boundaries of my ministry – even in retirement – so that I can be a blessing to others. And I can confidently say that the hand of God has indeed kept me from evil in a number of different ways.

If you are not already doing so, I suggest that you adapt the prayer of Jabez to your own particular situation – perhaps something like the prayer below – and start to use it as part of your own devotional prayer pattern today.

O Lord, I long for you to bless me indeed and to increase my effectiveness for your kingdom. May your hand be always with me to keep me from evil and let me be a blessing to others, causing them no pain. Amen

PAUL GRAVELLE

Ebed-melech: a random act of kindness?

Then the king commanded Ebed-melech, the Ethiopian, 'Take three men with you from here, and lift Jeremiah the prophet out of the cistern before he dies.' So Ebed-melech took the men with him and went… to a wardrobe of the storehouse, and took from there old rags and worn-out clothes… Then Ebed-melech the Ethiopian said to Jeremiah, 'Put the rags and clothes between your armpits and the ropes.' Jeremiah did so. Then they drew Jeremiah up with ropes and lifted him out of the cistern.

The Babylonians were at the gates and Jerusalem was divided. Some were prepared to seek help from Egypt but King Zedekiah was ready to surrender and Jeremiah knew that God had foretold Israel's defeat. The pro-Egyptian party, having had enough of Jeremiah's pronouncements, decided to keep him quiet – maybe permanently. But the Ethiopian Ebed-melech, a palace official, stepped in and, with the king's approval, effected a merciful – and comparatively comfortable – rescue.

Ebed-melech, a foreigner, far from his own country and not of the Jewish tradition, stepped out and performed this random act of kindness for the prophet Jeremiah at considerable risk to himself and at a time when his adoptive city was facing an uncertain future.

Although not a practising Jew, Ebed-melech had confidence that God would protect him. Jeremiah was given a specific prophetic word for him and, soon after his release from the cistern, passed this reassurance on to the Ethiopian: 'I will deliver you, says the Lord, and you shall not be given into the hand of the men of whom you are afraid… because you have put your trust in me' (Jeremiah 39:17–18).

In spite of the degenerate form of religion that prevailed around him, this stranger saw in Jeremiah's faithfulness to his God something that was trustworthy. So much so that he became a secret follower of Yahweh and was inspired to risk his own life to rescue God's prophet from a horrible death. Much more than a random act of kindness!

Can I trust God to protect me and calm my fears when I am confronted with an opportunity to serve him by going to the help of another?

PAUL GRAVELLE

Naaman's slave girl

Now Naaman was commander of the army of the king of Aram. He was a great man in the sight of his master and highly regarded, because through him the Lord had given victory to Aram. He was a valiant soldier, but he had leprosy. Now bands of raiders from Aram had gone out and had taken captive a young girl from Israel, and she served Naaman's wife. She said to her mistress, 'If only my master would see the prophet who is in Samaria! He would cure him of his leprosy.'

Aram was on Israel's northern border (in present-day Syria), so slavery of the kind described in today's passage was likely to have been a common occurrence. Cross-border raiding parties from various neighbouring states would have often taken captive and carried away Israelite women and girls. Naaman and his wife appear to have been benevolent slave owners, because the young Israelite girl was clearly concerned for her master's welfare and was not afraid to speak out about the effectiveness of the prophet Elisha's miraculous activities, as recorded in 2 Kings 4. She was a great witness!

Being a witness to what we have experienced of God's activity in our lives is a prime responsibility for all Christians. This is a frightening and daunting prospect for many of us, but the reward is great (Matthew 10:32) and, after all, this is why the Holy Spirit has been given: 'You will receive power when the Holy Spirit comes on you; and you will be my witnesses… to the ends of the earth' (Acts 1:8).

Here in New Zealand, we are conscious of the fact that we are indeed at 'the ends of the earth'. But wherever we are, we cannot escape Jesus' command to be witnesses to what he has done – and is doing – for us. I'm ashamed to say that I often miss opportunities to witness for Christ. Time after time I come away from a situation thinking, 'Oh, I should have said something about…' The little slave girl was not backward in coming forward. Should we not join her in this business of witnessing?

What is your most recent experience of God that you could share with someone else, given the right opportunity? Are you aware of the Holy Spirit's help in this?

PAUL GRAVELLE

Zechariah: rebuilding, God's way

Zechariah is a challenging book to read. It's written in that style we know as apocalyptic, which is quite foreign to us and can read like something from a science fiction novel rather than holy scripture. Graphic depictions loom up, so that we are confronted by visions that are as uncomfortable to us as they are hard to understand.

The book relates to the period after the destruction of Jerusalem and the exile of the majority of the people by the king of Babylon in 586BC. This period was marked by turmoil and uncertainty as prophets and writers struggled to understand what had happened to the nation and why God had seemingly abandoned them to a new slavery much like the agonies of their slavery in Egypt under Pharaoh.

It isn't clear that this book is the work of one person covering one period of time. Most commentators think that chapters 9—14 come from a later period. This means that fresh questions, visions and hopes are brought together, not in any random manner but because they present a fuller picture of what the future held for God's people.

However, it is a remarkable read and one that has deep significance for us today. To start, the prophet's name gives us a strong clue: Zechariah means 'God remembers'. The exiles wondered whether God had finally forgotten his promise to Abraham, because the nation's sin had been so great. Had they been utterly abandoned? The man and his message are all of a piece: God would restore and cleanse and renew the life of the nation and be Lord once more. Today the church faces similar challenges and therefore can draw strength from the message that God will be Lord and not defeated.

This book was as well known as the major prophets Jeremiah and Isaiah. It was therefore a part of scripture that was extremely important to Jesus and to the early Christian writers, who found in the coming of Jesus the fulfilment of all that Zechariah had foreseen. The book, like so much of the early scriptures, points us inevitably to the Lord Jesus Christ and how God had chosen him to be the longed-for salvation and hope for the whole world.

ANDREW BANGOR (ANDY JOHN)

On white horses

Therefore, thus says the Lord, I have returned to Jerusalem with compassion; my house shall be built in it, says the Lord of hosts, and the measuring line shall be stretched out over Jerusalem. Proclaim further: Thus says the Lord of hosts: My cities shall again overflow with prosperity; the Lord will again comfort Zion and again choose Jerusalem.

I am old enough to remember the black-and-white TV series *On White Horses*. It was a fairly gentle production, where you could guarantee a happy ending with galloping steeds coming to the rescue. It was quite different from the dramatic picture of red, sorrel and white horses patrolling the earth on God's behalf in this opening chapter. Here they are watchmen sent out to assess the moral and spiritual state of the whole world before reporting back to Almighty God.

Zechariah sets the scene for us: it's October 520BC and Darius' foreign and home policy has turned more favourably towards the exiles. This in no sense reduces the seriousness of the cause of that exile, which was unfaithfulness. However, the peace and calm identified by the equine messengers acts as a backdrop to the angelic prayer for mercy and clemency. And, of course, for God's change of heart. His compassion is aroused, much as it is in that better-known verse Isaiah 40:1. He will return to Jerusalem, comforting Zion and bringing prosperity and peace.

God longs to show favour to his people. Not cheaply, as though grace counted for naught, but rather because he is unwaveringly good and longs to restore what is broken. This message is at the heart of the gospel, because in Jesus we believe that God has done this very thing. When this same gospel becomes good news for us, it is transformative. We understand God's compassion for us, his unmerited favour and his deep longing for us to walk humbly before him. This is the hope that Zechariah begins to describe and to which we are invited to respond afresh today.

Father, you have ended the long years of exile through your Son, Jesus.
May I live as a free citizen of that heavenly city today, the new Jerusalem.
Amen

ANDY JOHN

Measuring line

I looked up and saw a man with a measuring line in his hand. Then I asked, 'Where are you going?' He answered me, 'To measure Jerusalem, to see what is its width and what is its length.' Then the angel who talked with me came forward, and another angel came forward to meet him and said to him, 'Run, say to that young man: Jerusalem shall be inhabited like villages without walls, because of the multitude of people and animals in it. For I will be a wall of fire all round it, says the Lord, and I will be the glory within it.'

I remember well the meticulous preparation of my father in his workshop. He knew where every tool belonged, and when a task presented itself his preparation for it was equally meticulous. To scrimp on the preparation time was to finish with substandard work. In chapter 2 of Zechariah, the prophet describes the work of preparation God undertakes for the return of the exiles. It possesses that same meticulous attention to detail. We begin with a man measuring the dimensions of the great city. It must be fit for purpose and ready to receive the Lord's redeemed. God will make space for himself in this place, as a wall of fire on the outside and glory within it. There is no place for the warmonger and oppressor, but the invitation is generous and urgent. Whole nations are invited to come and belong.

The New Testament contains many stories which involve preparation and invitation: the great day when we shall be gathered finally to our Father (Matthew 25:34); the preparation for the kingdom feast (Matthew 22:1–4); and the preparation of many rooms in John 14. The point here is that our homecoming has occupied God's attention. He has not scrimped but has been attentive and lavish, because his love and grace are beyond human expectation. Today we have an opportunity to recall the privilege of this invitation and the lengths to which our generous God has come to draw us to himself.

Lord God, you have done all things well and opened wide the gate for us to enter in. May we rejoice in your gracious invitation.

ANDY JOHN

Dressed for business

Now Joshua was dressed with filthy clothes as he stood before the angel. The angel said to those who were standing before him, 'Take off his filthy clothes.' And to him he said, 'See, I have taken your guilt away from you, and I will clothe you in festal apparel.' And I said, 'Let them put a clean turban on his head.' So they put a clean turban on his head and clothed him in the apparel; and the angel of the Lord was standing by.

Control of the exiles in this period lay with the local governor, a person of significance. Status would have been reflected in appropriate dress and wealth; their word would have commanded respect and fear. But here, it is not the governor who stands centre stage but the high priest Joshua. It comes as something of a shock to read how Joshua is clothed and that his rags have a deeper meaning, one associated with an inner uncleanness.

The work of preparation began with Jerusalem; it now turns to those who will teach and hold the vision of God's holiness. This role is assigned to the high priest, who will displace secular controls and administer the law impartially. But Joshua must be 'rightly clothed', not simply to indicate the dignity of office but to be righteous. Joshua can discharge his duty only if he is clean within. We can see how God was preparing for a new community whose lives would also need to be marked by holiness.

The Christian command to be clothed with Christ (Galatians 3:27) is closely connected with this thought. Here too, it is not a literal set of clothes so much as a picture of what should adorn our everyday lives – goodness, kindness and those other fruits of the Spirit named by Paul in his letter to the Galatians. The message is clear – no community can grow in love and grace if it is not clothed with, if it does not live each day in, those things that are from God.

Heavenly Father, as you clothed your servant in Zechariah's day, may we be clothed with those things that reflect the kingdom and holiness of your Son, Jesus, through whom we ask it. Amen

ANDY JOHN

Not by might

'What are you, O great mountain? Before Zerubbabel you shall become a plain…' Moreover, the word of the Lord came to me, saying, 'The hands of Zerubbabel have laid the foundation of this house; his hands shall also complete it. Then you will know that the Lord of hosts has sent me to you. For whoever has despised the day of small things shall rejoice, and shall see the plummet in the hands of Zerubbabel.'

I like the phrase 'corporate amnesia' (shared forgetfulness), but I also find it disturbing. It's one that is especially poignant today as we witness how society has forgotten its Christian history and story. Witness the numbers who do not know where Good Friday and even Easter Sunday originate!

One of the besetting sins of God's people in early times was forgetfulness. In Deuteronomy 8 we read the warnings given to those who are about to inherit the land and enjoy its bounty. The temptation for them is to enjoy the gifts and forget the giver. In chapter 4 of Zechariah, we read how the exchange between an angel and the prophet results in a strong reminder that the return of the exiles is the doing of God and none other (v. 6). God's people must not forget it is God who saves and restores us.

We have already noted that the restoration of the city was a key feature of the return of the exiles. The way this was carried out is described in the book of Nehemiah, which shows that a huge project to rebuild the city walls lay at the heart of what God commanded. Zechariah hints at this briefly here. He strengthens this vision by describing mountains laid low and buildings completed.

This is profoundly important for all of us who long to see change around us – in our churches and in our country. It is true that we must commit ourselves to doing the right things, but ultimately it is only God who can bring change. Today we have an opportunity to reflect on how God might bring this in situations we face, whether at home, at work or in the church.

Father, transform us by your Spirit so that what is real and lasting may be found in us. Amen

ANDY JOHN

The good life

Then the cover of lead was raised, and there in the basket sat a woman! He said, 'This is wickedness,' and he pushed her back into the basket and pushed its lead cover down on it. Then I looked up – and there before me were two women, with the wind in their wings! They had wings like those of a stork, and they lifted up the basket between heaven and earth.

In my early years as a curate, a local couple gave me their sofa. I did not have much furniture and was grateful for their generosity, but pulling the cushions from the base gave me some idea of their eating habits (note to reader: you really don't want to know). I suspect we have all had similar experiences and have wished we hadn't pulled the chest of drawers away from the wall or moved the fridge.

In this chapter, Zechariah wields two powerful pictures to emphasise there can be no rubbish in the lives of the redeemed: the scroll and the basket. The first is a warning against stealing and swearing falsely; the second, an admonition that all vice must be driven from the city. Wickedness has no place in this new environment. The message is similar: the new city demands a new life that is fitting and right for people to whom grace and mercy have come.

Zechariah's visions emphasise the fact that holiness points to what is true and authentic. Jesus taught that good fruit would be found only on good trees and bad fruit would be found only on what was diseased and decaying. This is of vital importance. Our behaviour is a sign of our faithfulness to God and an aspect of worship, reflecting commitment and devotion to God. It also shows we are serious about faith. It is easy to profess faith; it is another thing to demonstrate it by a Christ-like life. Lastly it speaks to the world when we are seen to be people who lead 'the good life' and whose honesty and integrity stand together.

Gracious God, turn our hearts again towards you so that we may live lives fitting the grace you have given to us in Jesus. Amen

ANDY JOHN

The rebuild

'The crown will be given to Heldai, Tobijah, Jedaiah and Hen son of Zephaniah as a memorial in the temple of the Lord. Those who are far away will come and help to build the temple of the Lord, and you will know that the Lord Almighty has sent me to you. This will happen if you diligently obey the Lord your God.'

Some recent work on the bishops' property where I am based involved detailed planning for health and safety with risk assessments, budgets and monitoring controls. It was instructive to see how different demands came together to complete the project. In this chapter, the picture of the proposed rebuild is fleshed out – but not the bricks and mortar so much as the other resources. Although the work of preparing for the return of the exiles was not systematic, it did include specific planning. In what way?

The prophecy identifies two resources vital for any successful plan: finance and people. Zechariah identifies the scattered exiles as a legitimate source of funding for the rebuild. Their silver and gold is to be used to make a new royal crown, which will symbolise a new kind of kingship. The reign of this new king – 'the Branch' – will extend God's reign far and wide. But the people are not just income-providers; they are the ones who will put grist to the mill and assist with the rebuild itself.

Elsewhere in the scriptures we see this unique connection of human and financial resources that is essential for any successful project. Paul makes a great deal of the way in which abundant giving involves abundant joy, and the impact of generosity on the human spirit (2 Corinthians 9:7). This should be the standard in all churches where resources, both money and personnel, enable the church to achieve good things and be a source of blessing. The challenge from today's reading centres on the extent to which we are willing to be abundant givers and joyful believers, and to realise the two are connected.

Generous Father, you have given us more than we could ask or imagine; give us hearts full of gratitude that overflow with thankfulness expressed in generous lives, for the sake of Jesus Christ. Amen

ANDY JOHN

A better law

And the word of the Lord came again to Zechariah: 'This is what the Lord Almighty said: "Administer true justice; show mercy and compassion to one another. Do not oppress the widow or the fatherless, the foreigner or the poor. Do not plot evil against each other."'

The problem was the T-Con board inside the TV. It wasn't broken but it was faulty and the consequence was a screen with psychedelic colours spiralling between images and text in a lurid way. It was the kind of thing of which migraines are made. Wonderfully, a new chip properly installed has seen the screen returned to full working order, and fewer headaches!

In today's reading we read of a flaw in the life of God's people, a fault that was partial but nonetheless serious and real. Its effect was to diminish life and worship even to the point of negating it. Our reading includes a command from God to put right this error and start again.

Firstly, the fault concerned the discipline of fasting and celebrating. Both were undertaken by God's people but in a way that did them no credit (7:5–6). Secondly a catalogue of omissions denied justice to those most in need. We have seen that rebuilding an environment fit for worship, life and faith lay at the heart of Zechariah's message. These two principles – putting God first and having an outward focus for faith – are a part of this same emphasis.

It is surely true that these are vital. If our worship lacks a sense of worth and sacrifice, it is cheapened and degraded and cannot please God. Likewise, the outward focus reminds us we are called to establish Jesus' kingdom of justice and peace. Today we are given an opportunity to reflect on what these things mean for our churches. How worthy and costly is the worship we offer each week, and how are we showing love and compassion? These are not extraneous to the things of God but lie at their heart.

Lord, teach us to worship and serve you as you would have us do in Jesus' name. Amen

ANDY JOHN

A new shalom

This is what the Lord Almighty says: 'Once again men and women of ripe old age will sit in the streets of Jerusalem, each of them with cane in hand because of their age. The city streets will be filled with boys and girls playing there.' This is what the Lord Almighty says: 'It may seem marvellous to the remnant of this people at that time, but will it seem marvellous to me?' declares the Lord Almighty.

I like the saying 'A vision without a plan is a dream. A plan without a vision is a chore.' In today's reading, Zechariah shifts the attention from expectations laid on God's people to promises God makes. It is a strong vision of hope and life restored. But this is no fantasy. The vision has a sound divine framework. In its richness and beauty, the vision must have encouraged those who heard it.

How would it have done this? Firstly, we are given a picture of what society looks like when God is Lord. It is one of complete transformation, where lawlessness gives way to harmony and peace. The old and young live together in mutual belonging and respect. Secondly, there is justice and safety, with wages properly paid and citizens living free from crime and fear of violence. Lastly, there is a renewal of material blessing, with crops producing enough for all.

It is tempting to set the vision of what might be against the reality of what is often experienced. But I have found that unless a purposeful vision inspires and directs us, we achieve very little.

Zechariah's vision laid out some of God's own hopes for the restored nation and how society could live justly and generously. What is challenging today is that the church is called to model these same principles and embrace this same vision. Our task is to show the reign of our God. This will involve vision and a plan.

Living God, you have called us to be light to the world. Give us wisdom to understand what this means in our day and to model the kind of society that offers hope to all, for Jesus' sake. Amen

ANDY JOHN

Prisoners of hope

Rejoice greatly, Daughter Zion! Shout, Daughter Jerusalem! See, your king comes to you, righteous and victorious, lowly and riding on a donkey, on a colt, the foal of a donkey. I will take away the chariots from Ephraim and the warhorses from Jerusalem and the battle bow will be broken. He will proclaim peace to the nations. His rule will extend from sea to sea and from the River to the ends of the earth.

Many of us will remember an advertisement for a mobile phone company which married a colour to a catchphrase: 'The future's bright.' It was a masterful piece of memory-making and made its appeal by connecting a product to a forward-looking perspective. Positive statements about the future are always powerful, and this is something Zechariah employs in this chapter.

We begin with a word to the nations who have oppressed the Hebrews: God's wrath has been kindled and they shall be humbled (vv. 1–4). The God who restores is just and shows no impartiality.

Our passage contains one of the most famous prophecies to find its way into the New Testament (Matthew 21:4–5). It shows how Jesus is the fulfilment of all the Hebrews have longed to see – and yet a very different king from the one many hoped would save and restore. It is easy to see how the Gospels found in these words the fulfilment of their deepest long-ings: the messiah king will bring the peace that has been denied them for so long. However, it is not merely an end to conflict that is envisaged but an extended reign of justice and prosperity (v. 16).

This new way of living is at the heart of the gospel. We have been res-cued from the dominion of darkness and the tyranny of sin, not to con-tinue within it but to live new and transformed lives. By this means the goodness and grace of God are revealed to the world. In this sense, the future really is bright and the best days are still to come.

Father, may your grace lead us to live lives worthy of you and your son,
Jesus. Amen

ANDY JOHN

Waves struck down

I will bring them back from Egypt and gather them from Assyria. I will bring them to Gilead and Lebanon, and there will not be room enough for them. They will pass through the sea of trouble; the surging sea will be subdued and all the depths of the Nile will dry up. Assyria's pride will be brought down and Egypt's sceptre will pass away.

I keep a shepherd's crook on the communion table in my chapel. Whenever I pray there or break bread with others, it reminds me of the task entrusted to me as a shepherd. The task is not to exercise a pastoral care that disempowers people but quite the opposite – one that enables them to make wise and responsible choices.

In today's chapter, the failure of the shepherds to look after the flock ignites God's anger (v. 3). It is because of the shepherds' neglect that the people wander and are aimless. They lack direction, so God resolves to be the shepherd himself and to undertake the task of leadership.

What should we make of today's reading? The astonishing message is that God does not need leaders to mediate his salvation. In fact, the elevation of God's people, whose shared life will show the gracious reign of God, displaces any role for the shepherds previously trusted to do this. This means it is God who delivers his great salvation and no other. When there is trouble ahead, it is God who will strike the surging sea and dry the threatening flood waters.

The effect of this is clear: salvation is God's sovereign right and needs no go-between. In the New Testament we read how the old system of sacrifice and mediation was essential to the life of God's people; without it we could not come to God completely (Hebrews 9:1–10). And the grace of God's sovereign salvation is foreshadowed here. It magnifies God's grace so that the praise is his alone. This gives us huge confidence, because if God is the author of our salvation, we may ask with Paul, 'Who is against us?' (Romans 8:31).

Father, all praise to you for showing us your strong and unshakeable salvation. May our confidence and trust in you never leave us. Amen.

ANDY JOHN

A worthless shepherd

This is what the Lord my God says: 'Shepherd the flock marked for slaughter. Their buyers slaughter them and go unpunished. Those who sell them say, 'Praise the Lord, I am rich!' Their own shepherds do not spare them. For I will no longer have pity on the people of the land,' declares the Lord. 'I will give everyone into the hands of their neighbours and their king. They will devastate the land, and I will not rescue anyone from their hands.'

You have probably heard the famous saying, 'Power corrupts, and absolute power corrupts absolutely'. It comes from Lord Acton, a British politician who used the phrase in 1887. Interestingly, he completed the sentence with these words: 'Great men are nearly always bad men.'

In today's reading we encounter some of the harshest words in the whole of the Old Testament. And that criticism is levelled at those who have exploited others for economic gain. In their pursuit of wealth, they have practised murder. Zechariah's savage commentary and his association with the very shepherds who are to be put to the sword leads to a dramatic word which annuls God's covenant and drives a wedge between the family ties of Judah and Israel.

There are two points to grasp. The first is how God's own justice is affronted when people exploit others. Such exploitation not only prevents society from performing its proper function but is contrary to God's will and purposes. We are not used to speaking about wrath, but it is a biblical concept (Romans 1:18) and underlines that God cannot be righteous if he remains unconcerned about a society's economic and moral well-being. Christian faith must address every area of life.

The second is that the dramatic end of fellowship between the nations of Judah and Israel and the withdrawal of God's favour (11:14, 10) paves the way for the Messiah, who will unite the nations. He too will be a shepherd, but a faithful and righteous one who lays down his life that they might live (John 10:11).

Father, let us see how your standards can be applied in the world
for the blessing of all people. Amen

ANDY JOHN

One they have pierced

'And I will pour out on the house of David and the inhabitants of Jerusalem a spirit of grace and supplication. They will look on me, the one they have pierced, and they will mourn for him as one mourns for an only child, and grieve bitterly for him as one grieves for a firstborn son. On that day the weeping in Jerusalem will be as great as the weeping of Hadad Rimmon in the plain of Megiddo.'

Today we find the prophet outlining the change that God's powerful intervention shall bring about. These are familiar themes, but they are given new meaning in the way Zechariah shows the new attitudes that will characterise life in the restored nation. Once more there is a tantalising reference to one whose gift, it would appear, is that he is frail and wounded. He would cause the people to mourn and weep. Such a figure points inevitably to the one whom we know was pierced for us (1 Peter 2:24).

Zechariah's vision is one in which justice prevails. The nations who destroyed Jerusalem, for example, are brought down and victory is given to Judah. It would be easy to understand this as a divine tit for tat – those who mete out violence are themselves subject to that same fate. Zechariah rather sees a new and dynamic shift in the way Jerusalem will live from this moment on. Firstly, they will possess a new compassion. Secondly, they will mourn and lament over the pierced one. This transformed outlook, in which arrogance is replaced by something softer, inevitably makes us think of both the beatitudes (Matthew 5:3–12) and the theme of weakness as a sign of true greatness seen in some of the epistles (for example, 2 Corinthians 12). It is remarkable that this Old Testament book should point us towards not only the Messiah's coming and how he will save us but also the way his death, here foreshadowed, should lead us to live holy lives.

Gracious Father, give us too hearts of compassion that are inspired by the one who was pierced for us. May we live lives worthy of him who gave himself for us. Amen

ANDY JOHN

Truth and honesty

'On that day a fountain will be opened to the house of David and the inhabitants of Jerusalem, to cleanse them from sin and impurity. On that day, I will banish the names of the idols from the land, and they will be remembered no more,' declares the Lord Almighty. 'I will remove both the prophets and the spirit of impurity from the land.'

You are probably familiar with the now common phrase 'fake news' and even with the computer programmes designed to spot the presence of this phenomenon. The 'post-truth' society seems to be relatively content with an outlook in which there are no timeless truths and nothing is certain.

In today's reading we learn there is little new about this. Truth has often been a casualty, but it is one from which God cannot turn and that he cannot ignore. The prophets and shepherds, those whom we might expect to hold the truth dear, receive particular censure.

God's remedy for this malaise is as radical as it is uncomfortable. Zechariah returns to a theme he has been exploring and presents three pictures to show how God will cleanse his people from this sin. He will do this, firstly, by water and washing; secondly, by removing the unclean spirit and falsehood; and thirdly, by refining through fire, which removes all impurities (v. 9). In the New Testament we see this same emphasis on cleansing from sin and cleaving to the truth. We cannot pretend at all with God; any claim to be free from sin is deceit (1 John 1:8–9). Jesus too spoke about the way truth sets us free to live the kind of life that brings joy and holiness (John 8:32). In both Testaments, God refuses to let error hold sway because this corrupts and distorts all relationships.

Today there is a fresh challenge to live truthfully and to be pure. Although this is direct and challenging, it is also hopeful, because this is the way in which God blesses us and by which we come to know God more deeply (v. 9).

Lord, teach us what it means to know the truth and to be set free to walk with you closely now and always. Amen

ANDY JOHN

King over the earth

On that day there will be neither sunlight nor cold, frosty darkness. It will be a unique day – a day known only to the Lord – with no distinction between day and night. When evening comes, there will be light. On that day living water will flow out from Jerusalem, half of it east to the Dead Sea and half of it west to the Mediterranean Sea, in summer and in winter. The Lord will be king over the whole earth. On that day there will be one Lord, and his name the only name.

This last chapter is a collection of sayings and a final word on the future of God's relationship with his people. It is also more strongly apocalyptic than the previous few chapters. At times it sounds similar to the last book in the New Testament, although it also draws on imagery used elsewhere in the Old Testament.

There are two themes we might note. The first is hope. Zechariah describes the final reign of God in rich and lavish language. There are neither dangers nor threats to God's people; they will live in safety and peace (v. 11). This vision is to give hope that God's rule will be glorious and blessed. This is not wishful thinking but establishes what life under God involves. The New Testament shares this great hope that God cannot be thwarted and that in Jesus God's reign has already begun (Mark 1:15).

The second theme is worship, in which the ancient festivals and place of Jerusalem are restored (v. 16). The practices long forgotten shall be restored and extended (v. 20) and holiness will again characterise the offering of God's people. Here, too, we might note how worship characterises life in the new Jerusalem and under God's reign (Revelation 4:11).

Perhaps it is fitting that Zechariah ends with worship, because worship is the trait that most of all marks people who love God and long for his presence and blessing. May this trait be ours in abundance.

Lord, give us hope that your future is good and blessed and a longing to worship you with every part of our being, in Jesus' name. Amen

ANDY JOHN

Words of encouragement and challenge

I have often heard it said that the words 'fear not' occur in the Bible 366 times, that is, once for every day of the year, even when it is a leap year. Recently I saw a discussion on social media as to whether this was actually true, and the majority opinion was that it was probably inaccurate. Nevertheless, the fact remains that the Bible is a source of rich encouragement, and time and again it reminds us that we have no need to be afraid.

In this series of readings we will be looking at some of the Bible's encouraging words, words designed to strengthen our faith and comfort us in the difficulties of life. Alongside these we will consider some other passages that contain more of a challenge, spurring us on to greater things and to a life of true discipleship.

These two words, encouragement and challenge, belong together. Encouragement without appropriate challenge can be mere soothsaying and leave us complacent; challenge without appropriate encouragement can be overly demanding and leave us disheartened. In reality we need both.

Here I have chosen both kinds of passages and interwoven them so that encouragement and challenge mingle freely together. Needless to say, my choice is subjective and far from exhaustive. I have shared scriptures that have impacted me over the years, whether by strengthening or by provoking me, and I hope they will speak to you as well.

Our English word 'encourage' comes from the French *encourager*, which means to make strong or to hearten. I enjoy watching sport, especially soccer, and am always intrigued to see how the coach encourages the players from the touchline. It is not always simply with words of sympathy and understanding; often it is with the challenge to do better, to try harder, to not give up. The coach wants to bring the best out of the team and spurs them on to greater endeavour.

My prayer is that as you read these notes you too will be encouraged in your faith and challenged to further growth in God.

TONY HORSFALL

Presence and purpose

Then Jesus came to them and said, 'All authority in heaven and on earth has been given to me. Therefore go and make disciples of all nations, baptising them in the name of the Father and of the Son and of the Holy Spirit, and teaching them to obey everything I have commanded you. And surely I am with you always, to the very end of the age.'

Here we have some of the last words of Jesus to his disciples, often referred to as the great commission because they outline the task set before the disciples – and all future generations of believers – once Jesus has returned to his Father in heaven: to take his message into the world, helping others to become his followers too. They present a significant challenge for the disciples but also offer sufficient encouragement for them to believe the task is not beyond them.

The church's mission involves going out into the world, crossing cultural boundaries and proclaiming the gospel message in ways that are relevant and engaging. The object is not to proselytise or gain new adherents, but to make disciples – people who will also follow the teachings of Jesus with sincere conviction. Such a calling is full of difficulty and requires a strong sense of being sent by God.

Two things make this possible. First, because Jesus has been given all authority, those who are sent in his name share in his power. They can expect him to back them up as they communicate his message, with God confirming the truth of what they proclaim, either through signs and wonders (Mark 16:15–18) or through powerful preaching (Luke 24:45–49).

Second, because they have the assurance of the risen presence of Jesus wherever they go. This promise is for all time (to the end of the age) and valid in all places (all nations). The words 'I am with you always' are often taken out of this context and made into a general promise, but rightly understood they apply best to those who have accepted the challenge of Jesus to go, and in obedience are seeking to make him known where he has sent them.

Lord, here indeed is a great challenge, but backed up with great promises.
May we as a church rise to the challenge.

TONY HORSFALL

The ever-present God

Keep your lives free from the love of money and be content with what you have, because God has said, 'Never will I leave you; never will I forsake you.' So we say with confidence, 'The Lord is my helper; I will not be afraid. What can mere mortals do to me?'

For many people money is the ground of their security. As long as they have money in the bank they feel secure, but the Bible warns against putting our trust in finances, which often prove unreliable. A focus on material wealth can make us avaricious and rob us of contentment. True security can be found only in God.

The writer reminds us of one of the most important promises that God has ever made to his people. He will never leave us and he will certainly never forsake us. Under no circumstances will he abandon us or let us down. This is to be the ground of our confidence. God can be trusted and is always with us.

It is likely that the words of Moses to the people of Israel, and to Joshua in particular, are in mind here. As Israel prepared to enter the promised land, Moses declared: 'he will never leave you nor forsake you' (Deuteronomy 31:6, 8). Crossing the Jordan and taking on the hostile tribes who inhabited the land was a daunting task, but Moses was convinced that since God had delivered his people in the past he would do so again in the future. His presence with them is assured, reminding them not to be afraid, and guaranteeing them success.

With this magnificent promise behind us, we can therefore join with the psalmist in making a bold assertion, that God is our helper and we need be afraid of no one (Psalm 118:6–7). What God has said becomes the reason for what we say, the confession of our faith. This is neither bravado nor presumption but boasting in the Lord.

Take hold of God's powerful statement today. He will never leave *you*; he will never forsake *you*. Let the faithfulness of God be the grounds of your confidence for whatever you are facing right now.

Lord, I rest on your word of encouragement: 'I am with you.'

TONY HORSFALL

Come and follow me

As Jesus walked beside the Sea of Galilee, he saw Simon and his brother Andrew casting a net into the lake, for they were fishermen. 'Come, follow me,' Jesus said, 'and I will send you out to fish for people.' At once they left their nets and followed him. When he had gone a little farther, he saw James son of Zebedee and his brother John in a boat, preparing their nets. Without delay he called them, and they left their father Zebedee in the boat with the hired men and followed him.

The Gospel accounts suggest that Jesus had previous contact with this group of fishermen, so their decision to follow him was not simply an impulsive act. It was still a brave decision, though, and one that would change their lives for ever.

The relationship between Jesus and his followers was patterned on that of a Jewish teacher and his disciples. His invitation to them is first to come and be apprenticed to him in order to learn from him. Jesus invites them to be with him so that they can share his life, watch him at work, listen to his teaching and follow his example. The objective is for them to become like him through the process of on-the-job training. It would require a high degree of commitment on their part, and also on his.

The second part of the invitation is to follow him. The mission of Jesus required him to criss-cross the country proclaiming the good news of the kingdom, and his disciples would be required to join him on his travels. This would mean their leaving their homes and families and giving up their jobs. It would involve a high degree of uncertainty and the need to trust God for their daily needs. That these four were willing to do this shows the depth of their attraction to the person of Jesus.

The call to discipleship has not changed. The requirements are just as demanding and the cost still as high. Jesus invites us to come to him and share his life, and then to follow wherever he leads us. Now there is a challenge.

Lord, I too have heard your call. Let me follow gladly in your footsteps.

TONY HORSFALL

I can do all things

I am not saying this because I am in need, for I have learned to be content whatever the circumstances. I know what it is to be in need, and I know what it is to have plenty. I have learned the secret of being content in any and every situation, whether well fed or hungry, whether living in plenty or in want. I can do all this through him who gives me strength.

Paul had a particularly close relationship with the church in Philippi. They were also fond of him and had often supported him financially in his ministry. A recent gift from them encouraged him and reminded him of a great lesson that God had taught him over the years: how to be content no matter what his circumstances.

One writer spoke of 'the rare jewel of Christian contentment', and most of us know what a struggle it is to be content with what we have (or don't have). We live in a consumerist world, where we are encouraged to be dissatisfied and to always look for something more, something better. We breathe an atmosphere of complaint, unrest and ingratitude that can infect the souls of even the godliest people. It seeps into our homes, our workplaces, even our churches.

Paul says that he has *learned* how to be content in his changing circumstances. That suggests that this was no overnight transformation but the result of a process taking place within him as the natural human tendency to grumble was replaced by a God-given ability to be grateful. Only the Holy Spirit can effect such a change.

That is why Paul acknowledges that the power behind his contentment came not from himself but from Christ: 'I can do all things through him who gives me strength' (v. 13). It is a promise that applies specifically to learning to be content, but can apply to any challenge that God sets before us. Whatever he asks us to do he will give us the strength to do it.

In the struggle you face today, remember this wonderful promise. God will give you the strength you need to act in a way that glorifies God.

Lord, release me from unhelpful dissatisfaction.
Teach me the joy of contentment.

TONY HORSFALL

Born of the Spirit

Jesus answered, 'Very truly I tell you, no one can enter the kingdom of God unless they are born of water and the Spirit. Flesh gives birth to flesh, but the Spirit gives birth to spirit. You should not be surprised at my saying, 'You must be born again.' The wind blows wherever it pleases. You hear its sound, but you cannot tell where it comes from or where it is going. So it is with everyone born of the Spirit.'

Here is another challenging statement from Jesus about being his follower: 'You must be born again.' There is no way round this requirement. Jesus insists that to enter the kingdom of God we must experience the new birth, the miracle of regeneration.

Nicodemus was a Pharisee, well-schooled in the intricacies and demands of the Jewish law. He was highly influential, sitting on the Sanhedrin, the Jewish ruling council, and yet he is clearly attracted to Jesus and his teaching. He is an honest seeker after truth, but struggles with this idea of being born again. His mind can only think in literal ways. 'How can someone be born when they are old?', he asks (v. 4).

Jesus of course is speaking about a second, spiritual birth. Just as we have a physical birth by which we enter the world, so we are to have a spiritual birth by which we enter God's kingdom. How this happens is both mysterious and miraculous. No one can fathom the process, just as we cannot really understand how the wind blows, yet the impact of it is life-changing – like starting all over again as a new person.

Despite Nicodemus' education and religious pedigree, Jesus holds him to this essential aspect of the kingdom. Even he needs to experience the new birth or he will be unable to live the new life for which Jesus calls.

The key to all this is given earlier in the Gospel: 'Yet to all who did receive him, to those who believed in his name, he gave the right to become children of God – children born not of natural descent, nor of human decision or a husband's will, but born of God' (John 1:12–13).

Lord, thank you for the possibility of a new life.

TONY HORSFALL

Grace that is sufficient

Therefore, in order to keep me from becoming conceited, I was given a thorn in my flesh, a messenger of Satan, to torment me. Three times I pleaded with the Lord to take it away from me. But he said to me, 'My grace is sufficient for you, for my power is made perfect in weakness.' Therefore I will boast all the more gladly about my weaknesses, so that Christ's power may rest on me. That is why, for Christ's sake, I delight in weaknesses, in insults, in hardships, in persecutions, in difficulties. For when I am weak, then I am strong.

Here are words to comfort the most troubled soul, words written out of Paul's own experience of suffering and pain that remind us of God's presence with us in our trials and his help in our times of need.

We are uncertain of the nature of Paul's affliction, but it is clearly physical, painful and persistent, something designed by Satan to frustrate and hinder him. Furthermore, Paul understandably wants to be free of the associated agony. His strategy is to pray, and to pray consistently, asking God to remove this thorn in his flesh. However, on this occasion, even the great apostle's prayers seem to be of no avail.

God's plan in this crisis is not to take the problem away but to give Paul sufficient strength to cope with the discomfort. The promise given to Paul is one that has strengthened God's people ever since, and one that is available still today: 'My grace is sufficient for you.'

Grace in this context speaks about God's strength being made available to us in our times of weakness or pain. The promise is that strength is not only available to us but given to us in a way that is sufficient for the circumstances in which we find ourselves. With this comes another extraordinary truth, that spiritual strength is best seen and displayed though human weakness: 'when I am weak, then I am strong.'

God may not always lift you out of your difficulties, but he will always give you the strength you need to live through them. There is both comfort and challenge.

Lord, I believe your promise. Your grace is sufficient for me.

TONY HORSFALL

Living sacrifices

Therefore, I urge you, brothers and sisters, in view of God's mercy, to offer your bodies as a living sacrifice, holy and pleasing to God – this is your true and proper worship. Do not conform to the pattern of this world, but be transformed by the renewing of your mind. Then you will be able to test and approve what God's will is – his good, pleasing and perfect will.

We are accustomed nowadays to think of worship in terms of music and liturgy and the things we do in our church services. This of course is perhaps the most common expression of worship, but it is far from being the complete picture. Paul exhorts his readers to remember that worship at its core involves the offering of one's self to God. Without this all outward forms of worship are empty.

'Wholehearted' is an apt description for the approach of Paul to life and ministry, and it is an attitude that he has in mind here. Halfheartedness has no place in his understanding of discipleship. To be real, discipleship requires the giving of one's self completely to God in order to do his will.

The idea of being a living sacrifice comes from Old Testament worship, in which the sacrifice of animals was a central practice. That system of worship has been fulfilled in Jesus, who offered himself as a once-for-all-time sacrifice for sin (Hebrews 9:26–28; 10:12). What God looks for now in true worship is not animal sacrifice but that the worshippers offer themselves completely to him in response to his prior love for them.

This is a great challenge, isn't it? Our instinct is to hold back and to keep control of our lives. We find the idea of surrendering our wills to another, even a God who loves us, difficult to accept and we fight against it. But remember what Paul says here: the will of God is in fact that which is best for us, to be embraced joyfully rather than resisted stubbornly. Why? Because it is what we were made for, and it leads to our deepest satisfaction and fulfilment.

Lord, why do I resist your will when all you want to do is to bless me?
Help me to surrender gladly to you.

TONY HORSFALL

God has plans for us

This is what the Lord says: 'When seventy years are completed for Babylon, I will come to you and fulfil my good promise to bring you back to this place. For I know the plans I have for you,' declares the Lord, 'plans to prosper you and not to harm you, plans to give you hope and a future. Then you will call on me and come and pray to me, and I will listen to you. You will seek me and find me when you seek me with all your heart.'

This is a word of grace to the Jewish exiles in Babylon, a promise of restoration to their homeland. Their repeated and persistent disobedience resulted in God's discipline whereby they were defeated by their enemies and taken away into captivity. Jeremiah, however, foretells a coming day when God will act again in mercy and bring them back to the promised land.

The exiles must have taken great heart from the realisation that God had not cast them aside and that he still had a purpose for them. His plans may have been disrupted, but they were certainly not defeated. These words give hope to us as well, for they reveal the character of God as one who has plans for his people and who brings those purposes to pass despite our weakness and failure.

God knows the plans he has for us. We may feel confused by life events, and wonder what is happening, but God hasn't lost the plot. Even if it takes a long time, his perfect will for us is being worked out.

God has good plans for us. When we realise this we can be confident in the present and optimistic for the future, and we can dare to trust him with our lives. He wants to do what is best for us, not harm us.

What God desires more than anything is that we should live in relationship with him. He longs for us to connect with him through prayer, and to get to know him more deeply and intimately. When we choose to seek him sincerely we can be sure that we shall find the reality of his presence.

Lord, I thank you that you have a plan for my life.

TONY HORSFALL

Live a life of love

Be kind and compassionate to one another, forgiving each other, just as in Christ God forgave you. Follow God's example, therefore, as dearly loved children and walk in the way of love, just as Christ loved us and gave himself up for us as a fragrant offering and sacrifice to God.

To suggest that we are called to live a life of love may not seem at first sight like a difficult assignment, until we realise how unloving we are and how hard it is to love some people! As an ideal, loving others is great, and in a perfect world it might be possible, but it proves to be a big challenge when we live in the real world with real people.

Paul's words to the church at Ephesus contain two encouragements to help us walk this difficult path. The first is the recognition that we ourselves, with all our faults and failings, are loved by God. Christ demonstrated the greatness of God's love when he went to the cross and paid the penalty for our sins. That is the definitive proof of God's love and there is no need for anyone to doubt that they are loved by God, however unworthy they may feel (Romans 5:8). Here is a spiritual dynamic: knowing we ourselves are loved enables us then to love others and to demonstrate the same selflessness that Christ showed when he went to the cross.

The second encouragement is to ponder the gift of forgiveness that we have received as a result of Christ's death, a forgiveness that is total and free and completely undeserved. Again, knowing we have been forgiven so much ourselves releases a spiritual dynamic into our lives that makes us more compassionate towards others and their failures. It enables us to forgive those who have sinned against us.

Let's not pretend that loving others is easy. It isn't, and we require all the help that God offers to us through the work of his enabling Spirit within us. Meditating on the greatness of God's love towards us and pondering the generosity of his wonderful forgiveness will prepare the soil of our hearts to receive the seeds of that divine love.

Lord, make me a more loving person, kind and compassionate.

TONY HORSFALL

God working all things for good

And we know that in all things God works for the good of those who love him, who have been called according to his purpose. For those God foreknew he also predestined to be conformed to the image of his Son, that he might be the firstborn among many brothers and sisters.

Here is another truth that has always encouraged God's people: God has the ability to weave whatever happens to us into his overall good purpose. That purpose is that we might become like Jesus in our character, attitudes, words and actions. Such a transformation takes place in the midst of everyday life and is brought about largely by the way God uses circumstances to shape us.

'All things' is a comprehensive description, suggesting that nothing is outside the control of God. This does not mean that all things are good or that those things by themselves work for our good. The truth is that many things happen in this world that are not directly God's will. They are the result of human sinfulness and happen because we live in a fallen world where the created order itself has been thrown into chaos. God has given us a measure of freedom, and sometimes we use that freedom to act in wrong ways, damaging ourselves and others.

Yet here is the great truth. God can take all the mess we create and turn it around for our ultimate good. He can use suffering to form character within us, making us more humble and compassionate (Romans 5:3–4). He can take the good and the bad that come our way and weave both together to create a beautiful tapestry of our lives.

Joseph was thrown into a pit and left to die by his brothers, sold into slavery in Egypt and then unjustly imprisoned before being released into the service of Pharaoh. There he became a powerful official who was able to help his brothers when they came to Egypt for food. With the perspective of hindsight and a measure of faith, he saw this principle at work. He told them, 'You intended to harm me, but God intended it for good' (Genesis 50:20).

Lord, help me to grasp this truth and to see your guiding hand in my life.

TONY HORSFALL

Faith without works?

What good is it, my brothers and sisters, if someone claims to have faith but has no deeds? Can such faith save them? Suppose a brother or a sister is without clothes and daily food. If one of you says to them, 'Go in peace; keep warm and well fed,' but does nothing about their physical needs, what good is it? In the same way, faith by itself, if it is not accompanied by action, is dead.

The epistle of James is perhaps the most practical and down-to-earth of all the books in the New Testament. Here we find a vision for the Christian life where faith is lived out in everyday, tangible ways in society, not hidden away behind church doors. That is where the challenge lies. It is easy to adopt an individualised private faith that, while comforting in itself, makes no positive impact on others. James is very clear, however. Faith without an outward expression is not real faith. It is dead.

For example, it is not sufficient to treat those in need with pious platitudes, wishing them well but doing nothing to alleviate their suffering. Rather, if we see someone in need and we have the resources and opportunity to meet that need then we are responsible before God for doing something to help. Faith has to lead to action, otherwise it is barren.

True faith can never be either passive or hidden; it must be expressed in our actions. The world around us needs to see faith in action both to confirm the veracity of that faith and to demonstrate that God does care for those in need. It is a great joy to see Christians increasingly at the forefront of social action: running food banks, organising shelters for the homeless, working as street pastors, setting up mums-and-toddler groups, caring for refugees and so on – ordinary people being involved in helping others simply because they want to share the love of God.

Every believer can ask God to show them a way in which they can express their faith to benefit others. It need not be grand, just a simple way of putting faith into action however we can.

Lord, help me to be more outward-looking and to live my faith practically.

TONY HORSFALL

Peace that surpasses all understanding

Rejoice in the Lord always. I will say it again: Rejoice! Let your gentleness be evident to all. The Lord is near. Do not be anxious about anything, but in every situation, by prayer and petition, with thanksgiving, present your requests to God. And the peace of God, which transcends all understanding, will guard your hearts and your minds in Christ Jesus.

Paul's letter to the Philippians has been called the epistle of joy since it carries such a positive note. Here we are reminded that Christians of all people have good reason to be glad: the presence of God is always with them.

Anxiety is one of the crippling characteristics of contemporary society. Life in a fast-paced and increasingly complex world is hard to manage, and the stresses and strains are seen in growing numbers of people of all ages suffering mental illness. Paul reminds us that there is a spiritual antidote for anxiety, whatever its source – the healing value of a prayerful relationship with God.

Prayer is the means by which we can communicate with God, and we are invited to bring all our needs to him, asking for his help and intervention. This we can do with confidence that God is listening and that we can be honest and open with him about our concerns. That in itself is therapeutic, but there is more.

Paul reminds us that as we unburden ourselves to God we will begin to receive the peace of God that will calm our minds (from restless thoughts) and our hearts (from troublesome emotions). This happens as we hand over our concerns to God and trust that he has heard our requests: 'Cast all your anxiety on him because he cares for you' (1 Peter 5:7).

Worry changes nothing but robs us of our joy and peace. Most of what we worry about never comes to pass anyway. We may feel that if we truly care we ought to worry, but worrying will make no difference. Trust is what is required, and then we can know peace, which will help us to deal more effectively with what concerns us.

Lord, teach me to trust and to hand over to your safe keeping the things that trouble me.

TONY HORSFALL

Micah's challenge

With what shall I come before the Lord and bow down before the exalted God? Shall I come before him with burnt offerings, with calves a year old? Will the Lord be pleased with thousands of rams, with ten thousand rivers of olive oil? Shall I offer my firstborn for my transgression, the fruit of my body for the sin of my soul? He has shown you, O mortal, what is good. And what does the Lord require of you? To act justly and to love mercy and to walk humbly with your God.

The Old Testament prophet Micah was a contemporary of Isaiah, Amos and Hosea. Like them he called for social justice as the true expression of worship, declaring that we serve God best by doing what is right and fair.

Inspired by these words, the Micah Challenge came into being in the 1990s, a worldwide coalition of Christian organisations with a common concern to unite Christians to fight global poverty and to seek justice for the poor. Its aim is to take seriously these words of the prophet Micah, encouraging believers to learn about the issues behind poverty, to find ways themselves to help the poor and to fight for justice.

The church has always had a social conscience. We think of the work of William Wilberforce and the abolition of slavery, Robert Raikes and the Sunday School movement or William Booth and the social work of the Salvation Army. These pioneers were remarkable people, and we may not feel capable of such great works ourselves. Micah, however, brings the challenge down to the level of ordinary individuals, and asks us to think about how we live and the values that guide us – in other words to develop a personal social conscience.

We are to be concerned for justice, not only for ourselves but for others also. This may mean campaigning for those who have no voice or standing against policies that adversely affect the most vulnerable.

We are to love mercy, which will involve us in compassionate action, either by personal involvement or by prayer and financial support.

Finally, we are to walk humbly with God, living out our faith in daily life.

Lord, soften my heart and make me responsive to the need around me.

TONY HORSFALL

This page is left blank for your notes

Reading *New Daylight* in a group

SALLY WELCH

I am aware that although some of you cherish the moments of quiet during the day that enable you to read and reflect on the passages we offer you in *New Daylight*, other readers prefer to study in small groups, to enable conversation and discussion and the sharing of insights. With this in mind, here are some ideas for discussion starters within a study group. Some of the questions are generic and can be applied to any set of contributions within this issue; others are specific to certain sets of readings. I hope they generate some interesting reflections and conversations!

General discussion starters

These questions can be used for any study series within this issue. Remember, there are no right or wrong answers; they are intended simply to enable a group to engage in conversation.

- What do you think the main idea or theme of the author is in this series? Do you think they succeeded in communicating this to you, or were you more interested in the side issues?

- Have you had any experience of the issues that are raised in the study? How have they affected your life?

- What evidence does the author use to support their ideas? Do they use personal observations and experience, facts, quotations from other authorities? Which appeals to you most?

- Does the author make a 'call to action'? Is that call realistic and achievable? Do you think their ideas will work in the secular world?

- Can you identify specific passages that struck you personally – as interesting, profound, difficult to understand or illuminating?

- Did you learn something new reading this series? Will you think differently about some things, and if so, what are they?

Zechariah (Andy John)

Andy talks about corporate amnesia, or shared forgetfulness, with reference to today's society forgetting its Christian heritage. What examples do you see of that in your own experience? Do you think your church community suffers from corporate amnesia with reference to certain aspects of the Christian tradition? What is your church's original purpose and how might you encourage your community to recollect it? Have you ever witnessed the power of a crowd? Was it for good or evil? Have you ever joined in with a crowd, such as at a political demonstration or a musical event? How did this feel?

1 Samuel (Bob Mayo)

Bob writes that God works through people when they are in vulnerable situations. Has this been your experience? Has your faith helped you to remain strong or have you felt God work when you are at your weakest? What would you say to encourage others who are feeling vulnerable?

Reflective question (Favourite prayers, Sally Welch)

Pilgrims have to travel light if they are to make a successful journey. What are the essentials you take with you? Consider both material things and those to help you on your spiritual journey.

God of our pilgrimage

Author profile: Paul Gravelle

How long have you been an Anglican priest, and what first inspired you to seek ordination?

I was ordained in 1977, so celebrated my 40th anniversary last year. One Sunday, listening to a very boring sermon, I 'heard a voice in my head' (that is the only way I can describe it) saying, 'You will do better than this for me.'

You have ministered in military, urban and rural settings. What have these been like?

As you can imagine there have been challenges and joys in each of these situations. However, military chaplaincy has offered the most challenges and my current urban ministry the most joys. I should say, too, that my years in a rural setting have faced me with the most comic situations, but they don't really count as joys!

You lead retreats and workshops, where you are face-to-face with your audience. How have you found the experience of writing for people you can't see?

Imagination goes a long way in this. When writing, I always find myself envisaging my future readers and trying to sense their reactions. I also subject my long-suffering wife to a trial run and do my best to respond to her critique. I have no illusions about my qualities as a speaker and am much more comfortable with writing. I have just published *The Village*, a short story for senior citizens entirely in verse which presents the Christian gospel in an initially comic situation. It seems to be hitting the spot!

Which spiritual writers have influenced you and in what ways?

C.S. Lewis has always been my great hero, but Tom Wright, Francis MacNutt, Arnold Bittlinger and Nicky Gumbel of the Alpha course have been among those who have influenced both my writing and speaking. Lewis and Gumbel have both helped to clarify my faith journey and provided me with the tools to communicate that faith to others. Bittlinger and MacNutt have unpacked the practicalities of spiritual gifts for me in ways that have added new dimensions to my ministry.

Recommended reading

Jesus encouraged the disciples to eat within the community, build friendships, make contacts and teach the gospel. In *Eat, Pray, Tell*, Andrew Francis urges us to notice the order. The disciples were to seek the welfare of others by praying for and healing them – in other words, by meeting their obvious needs. It was only then that teaching and telling about the 'reign of God' would begin. This was Jesus' strategy for mission. Andrew Francis suggests that it should be ours today. The following extract is taken from the Introduction.

'Eat, pray, tell...'

It takes a hard heart to resist the image often seen on film or TV of large Mediterranean families gathered on a sun-drenched terrace, laughing and eating around a well-stocked table. How many holiday-makers who venture beyond the confines of their package-tour hotel return with stories of shared meals and others' rich hospitality? That traditional pattern of life is part of a culture stretching the length of the Mediterranean and back through Levantine history. Any reader of the classics or the Bible can find many reminders that a life involving the sharing of food was part of those cultural histories.

At the end of his earthly ministry, just before his ascension into heaven, Matthew tells of Jesus' great commission: 'Go and make disciples of all nations, baptising them... and teaching them...' (Matthew 28:19–20). Many Christians today are wrestling with how to exercise that mission today. We need to (re)discover a relevant model that works in our culture now as clearly as it did for the apostles and the early church after the first Pentecost. For without mission, the Christian community will die.

Sometimes, when speaking at a conference, I invite the audience to break into small groups and share with each other the best moments in their lives. While some people will rank a solo experience as their best – standing alone on a mountain peak at sunrise or some moment of great courage or skill (or even rank stupidity) – the vast majority of people quickly recall a time that involved eating with others. Indeed, the best conversations at such conferences come not from the seminar room but over the meal tables or in the afternoon queue for tea and scones. Our listening and learning is enhanced as we eat together.

When travelling solo across the USA between speaking appointments, I hardly ever visit a diner without someone sharing my booth and engaging me in conversation while we eat. In several of my other books, I document my similar experiences of hospitality and meal-sharing across the world, from the Americas through the Mediterranean islands to the Far East. When developing a retreat house ministry in France, I adopted the rich patterns of local hospitality, echoed in the Bible, to enable our guests – both friends and strangers – to feel welcome.

I say all this to encourage you that your life's journey and everyday experiences can enable you to reflect on Jesus' eat-pray-tell pattern of mission, and to realise this is just as relevant today.

Learning from Jesus's earthly ministry

Jesus told his disciples, 'Whatever town or village you enter, find out who in it is worthy, and stay there until you leave' (Matthew 10:11; see also Mark 6:8–13; Luke 9:1–6). That is, eating within the community would help the disciples to establish local contacts, build friendships and create bonds of trust. The disciples were then to seek the welfare of others by praying for and healing them; in other words, meeting their obvious and self-declared needs. It was only then that teaching and telling about the 'reign of God' would begin.

Jesus could hardly have advocated this pattern without the social mores of his time involving the practice of hospitality. People would welcome newcomers, whether friend or stranger, to their homes with a meal and space to sleep. Except in the worst weather, such a daily meal would normally have been outdoors and a sheltered corner of a courtyard would have been secure enough to safely sleep in.

Within the New Testament, the Gospels provide us with different written representations of the life of Jesus and his first followers, who came to be called Christians. The four Gospels provide us with four different portraits of Jesus. Matthew, Mark and Luke give similar portraits, because they share a similar viewpoint; scholars call these three Gospels the synoptics, from the Greek meaning 'with one view' (or literally 'with one eye'). The Gospel of John comes from almost a generation later, drawing on a different community which was heavily influenced by Greek philosophical thought. It is hardly surprising, therefore, that the Gospels give us helpfully contrasting patterns of meals in the early Christian communities.

Despite their different perspectives, all the Gospels have a variety of references to Jesus eating with both his disciples and with others, such as Zacchaeus the collaborating tax collector (Luke 19:1–10) or the unnamed Pharisee (Luke 14:7–14). Moreover, two of the few episodes that are recorded in all four Gospels, although with variations on the details, refer to shared meals: the feeding of the multitude (Matthew 14:13–21; Mark 6:30–44; Luke 9:10–17; John 6:5–13) and the last supper (Matthew 26:17–30; Mark 14:12–25; Luke 22:7–23; John 13:1–30). Narratives of shared meals, therefore, are a central part of the Gospels' trajectory, and the feeding of the multitude and the last supper, in particular, demonstrate how 'eating together' declares the 'reign of God'.

When it comes to the rest of the New Testament, consider how often the various writers of the letters send greetings to churches by name. Such relationships would not have occurred instantly but only over time, living and ministering together, which would have naturally involved several meals and conversation. Eating together helps us build relationships within the Christian community – however diverse and in however many congregations. Part of my rich joy in travelling to different churches to preach or to speak at conferences is to share in the hospitality of others' homes.

In the 21st century, we must heed Jesus' way of doing things, but we have to recognise that our society has different cultural norms and avoid placing ourselves and others at risk as we consider an eat-pray-tell ministry. Another purpose of this book, in its later chapters, is to offer you the example and encouragement of others who are working out their eat-pray-tell reflections in practical ways.

What this means for us now

Why does this practical strategy have application for the contemporary Western church? In recent years, there has been a significant growth of literature re-examining how the practice, lifestyle and spirituality of the early church can help us live faithfully as Christians in multicultural Britain (and other countries). In many communities and regions in what was once called Christendom, the church is becoming increasingly marginalised. Fewer and fewer people have any real understanding of the Bible, of the Christian origins of our customs and festivals, or what it means to be a Christian. Many commentators and academics regard the West today as being in an era of post-Christendom.

We briefly reviewed above how shared meals are a common denominator across many cultures and were a central feature of the life and mission of Jesus and the early church, as narrated in the Gospels and New Testament letters. We can learn from the life of Mediterranean communities and church history how our festivals and faith gather both the enquirer and the faithful through the melange of hospitality, community and prayer.

My own life has been richly flavoured by many different experiences within different expressions of Jesus' radical communities. Looking back, I realise what a debt I owe to those Franciscan and Mennonite houses of welcome, to the influence of South American liberation theologians and northern hemisphere eco-feminist theologians, as well as the communities of Taizé and Iona. I have also had heroes of mine, such as Archbishop Tutu or Thomas Merton, who along with my spiritual directors helped me understand how prayer and activism must intertwine. My eat-pray-tell education was often around others' tables – so some of these encounters appear in the following pages.

We have to find ways in which others have had vibrant and transformative Christian experiences, learn from those ways and apply what we have learned in our own context, congregation and neighbourhood. In Britain, particularly in the cities, it is not hard to find someone who has been on an Alpha course. Often, whatever else their experience of the course, they will speak of a sense of welcome at the shared meal and of being listened to. Equally, in many cities, towns and suburbs, you can quickly discover those who have encountered the hospitality of Messy Church. You do not have to go far into the life of the church to realise that, despite problems with the church building, the mockery of TV comedians or the antagonism of the media in general, Christians have things to say that are relevant, life-changing and creative. Vibrant prayer and rich spirituality are far more prevalent than dry rot in British churches!

To order a copy of this book, please use the order form on the facing page.

To order

Delivery times within the UK are normally
15 working days. Prices are correct at the time of
going to press but may change without prior notice.

Title	Price	Qty	Total
Eat, Pray, Tell	£7.99		
God among the Ruins	£7.99		
Faith in the Making	£7.99		

POSTAGE AND PACKING CHARGES			
Order value	UK	Europe	Rest of world
Under £7.00	£2.00	£5.00	£7.00
£7.00–£29.99	£3.00	£9.00	£15.00
£30.00 and over	FREE	£9.00 + 15% of order value	£15.00 + 20% of order value

Total value of books	
Postage and packing	
Total for this order	

Please complete in BLOCK CAPITALS

Title .... First name/initials .... Surname ....

Address ....

.... Postcode ....

Acc. No. .... Telephone ....

Email ....

❑ Please keep me informed by email about BRF's books and resources
❑ Please keep me informed by email about the wider work of BRF

Method of payment

❑ Cheque (made payable to BRF) ❑ MasterCard / Visa

Card no. ▢▢▢▢ ▢▢▢▢ ▢▢▢▢ ▢▢▢▢ ▢▢▢▢ ▢▢▢▢

Valid from ▢▢ ▢▢ Expires ▢▢ ▢▢ Security code* ▢▢▢
Last 3 digits on the reverse of the card

Signature* .... Date .... /............ /............

*ESSENTIAL IN ORDER TO PROCESS YOUR ORDER

Please return this form to: BRF, 15 The Chambers, Vineyard, Abingdon OX14 3FE | enquiries@brf.org.uk
To read our terms and find out about cancelling your order, please visit **brfonline.org.uk/terms**.

The Bible Reading Fellowship (BRF) is a Registered Charity (233280)

How to encourage Bible reading in your church

BRF has been helping individuals connect with the Bible for over 90 years. We want to support churches as they seek to encourage church members into regular Bible reading.

Order a Bible reading resources pack

This pack is designed to give your church the tools to publicise our Bible reading notes. It includes:

- Sample Bible reading notes for your congregation to try.
- Publicity resources, including a poster.
- A church magazine feature about Bible reading notes.

The pack is free, but we welcome a £5 donation to cover the cost of postage. If you require a pack to be sent outside the UK or require a specific number of sample Bible reading notes, please contact us for postage costs. More information about what the current pack contains is available on our website.

How to order and find out more

- Visit **biblereadingnotes.org.uk/for-churches**
- Telephone BRF on +44 (0)1865 319700 Mon–Fri 9.15–17.30
- Write to us at BRF, 15 The Chambers, Vineyard, Abingdon OX14 3FE

Keep informed about our latest initiatives

We are continuing to develop resources to help churches encourage people into regular Bible reading, wherever they are on their journey. Join our email list at **biblereadingnotes.org.uk/helpingchurches** to stay informed about the latest initiatives that your church could benefit from.

Introduce a friend to our notes

We can send information about our notes and current prices for you to pass on. Please contact us.

Transforming lives and communities

BRF is a charity that is passionate about making a difference through the Christian faith. We want to see lives and communities transformed through our creative programmes and resources for individuals, churches and schools. We are doing this by resourcing:

- **Christian growth and understanding of the Bible.** Through our Bible reading notes, books, digital resources, Quiet Days and other events, we're resourcing individuals, groups and leaders in churches for their own spiritual journey and for their ministry.
- **Church outreach in the local community.** BRF is the home of three programmes that churches are embracing to great effect as they seek to engage with their local communities: Messy Church, Who Let The Dads Out? and The Gift of Years.
- **Teaching Christianity in primary schools.** Our Barnabas in Schools team is working with primary-aged children and their teachers, enabling them to explore Christianity creatively and confidently within the school curriculum.
- **Children's and family ministry.** Through our Parenting for Faith programme, websites and published resources, we're working with churches and families, enabling children and adults alike to explore Christianity creatively and bring the Bible alive.

Do you share our vision?

Sales of our books and Bible reading notes cover the cost of producing them. However, our other programmes are funded primarily by donations, grants and legacies. If you share our vision, would you help us to transform even more lives and communities? Your prayers and financial support are vital for the work that we do.

- You could support BRF's ministry with a one-off gift or regular donation (using the response form on page 153).
- You could consider making a bequest to BRF in your will (page 152).
- You could encourage your church to support BRF as part of your church's giving to home mission – perhaps focusing on a specific area of our ministry, or a particular member of our Barnabas in Schools team.
- Most important of all, you could support BRF with your prayers.

Make a lasting difference through a gift in your will

The humble match is a wonder of modern invention. Since the dawn of time humanity had tried to create and harness fire, but nobody came close to finding a reliable self-igniting source until 1805, when the first match was struck. Now just a quick flick along a rough surface is enough to create a spark. Under the right conditions, this will grow into a powerful fire.

BRF's story began in a similar way in 1922, with a spark of an idea and the vision of just one man. Revd Leslie Mannering wanted to help his congregation 'get a move on spiritually'. His idea spread like wildfire and soon BRF was born, a charity committed to transforming lives and communities through the Christian faith.

With God's help, we've fanned the flames for over 90 years and have seen our impact grow. Today we are now home to four programmes that churches worldwide are embracing as they seek to engage with local communities and transform lives: Messy Church, The Gift of Years, Who Let The Dads Out? and Parenting for Faith. Messy Church, in particular, is an outstanding success story. Our network of nearly 4,000 Messy Churches reaches an estimated 500,000 people each month with the good news of Jesus Christ.

If you share our passion for making a difference through the Christian faith, would you consider leaving a gift to BRF in your will? Gifts in wills are an important source of income for us and they don't need to be huge to make a real difference. For every £1 we receive, we invest 95p back into charitable activities. Just imagine what we could do over the next century with your help.

For further information about making a gift to BRF in your will, please visit **brf.org.uk/lastingdifference**, contact Sophie Aldred on **+44 (0)1865 319700** or email **giving@brf.org.uk**.

Whatever you can do or give, we thank you for your support.

SHARING OUR VISION – MAKING A GIFT

I would like to make a gift to support BRF. Please use my gift for:

☐ where it is needed most ☐ Barnabas in Schools ☐ Parenting for Faith
☐ Messy Church ☐ Who Let The Dads Out? ☐ The Gift of Years

Title	First name/initials	Surname	
Address			
			Postcode
Email			
Telephone			
Signature			Date

giftaid it You can add an extra 25p to every £1 you give.

Please treat as Gift Aid donations all qualifying gifts of money made

☐ today, ☐ in the past four years, ☐ and in the future.

I am a UK taxpayer and understand that if I pay less Income Tax and/or Capital Gains Tax in the current tax year than the amount of Gift Aid claimed on all my donations, it is my responsibility to pay any difference.

☐ My donation does not qualify for Gift Aid.

Please notify BRF if you want to cancel this Gift Aid declaration, change your name or home address, or no longer pay sufficient tax on your income and/or capital gains.

Please complete other side of form ➡

Please return this form to:
BRF, 15 The Chambers, Vineyard, Abingdon OX14 3FE

BRF

The Bible Reading Fellowship is a Registered Charity (233280)

SHARING OUR VISION – MAKING A GIFT

Regular giving

By Direct Debit:

☐ I would like to make a regular gift of £ [____] per month/quarter/year.
Please also complete the Direct Debit instruction on page 159.

By Standing Order:

Please contact Priscilla Kew +44 (0)1235 462305 | giving@brf.org.uk

One-off donation

Please accept my gift of:

☐ £10 ☐ £50 ☐ £100 Other £ [____]

by (delete as appropriate):

☐ Cheque/Charity Voucher payable to 'BRF'

☐ MasterCard/Visa/Debit card/Charity card

Name on card

Card no. [   ] [   ] [   ] [   ]

Valid from [M M] [Y Y] Expires [M M] [Y Y]

Security code* [   ] *Last 3 digits on the reverse of the card
ESSENTIAL IN ORDER TO PROCESS YOUR PAYMENT

Signature   Date

We like to acknowledge all donations. However, if you do not wish to receive an acknowledgement, please tick here ☐

↩ Please complete other side of form

Please return this form to:
BRF, 15 The Chambers, Vineyard, Abingdon OX14 3FE

BRF

The Bible Reading Fellowship is a Registered Charity (233280)

ND0218

NEW DAYLIGHT SUBSCRIPTION RATES

Please note our new subscription rates, current until 30 April 2019:

Individual subscriptions
covering 3 issues for under 5 copies, payable in advance
(including postage & packing):

	UK	Europe	Rest of world
New Daylight	£16.95	£25.20	£29.10
New Daylight 3-year subscription (9 issues) (not available for Deluxe)	£46.35	N/A	N/A
New Daylight Deluxe per set of 3 issues p.a.	£21.45	£32.25	£38.25

Group subscriptions
covering 3 issues for 5 copies or more, sent to **one** UK address (post free):

New Daylight	£13.50 per set of 3 issues p.a.
New Daylight Deluxe	£17.25 per set of 3 issues p.a.

Please note that the annual billing period for group subscriptions runs from 1 May to 30 April.

Overseas group subscription rates
Available on request. Please email **enquiries@brf.org.uk**.

Copies may also be obtained from Christian bookshops:

New Daylight	£4.50 per copy
New Daylight Deluxe	£5.75 per copy

All our Bible reading notes can be ordered online by visiting
biblereadingnotes.org.uk/subscriptions

For information about our other Bible reading notes,
and apps for iPhone and iPod touch, visit
biblereadingnotes.org.uk

NEW DAYLIGHT INDIVIDUAL SUBSCRIPTION FORM

All our Bible reading notes can be ordered online by visiting
biblereadingnotes.org.uk/subscriptions

☐ I would like to take out a subscription:

Title .... First name/initials .... Surname ....

Address ....

.... Postcode ....

Telephone .... Email ....

Please send *New Daylight* beginning with the September 2018 / January 2019 / May 2019 issue (*delete as appropriate*):

(please tick box)	UK	Europe	Rest of world
New Daylight 1-year subscription	☐ £16.95	☐ £25.20	☐ £29.10
New Daylight 3-year subscription	☐ £46.35	N/A	N/A
New Daylight Deluxe	☐ £21.45	☐ £32.25	☐ £38.25

Total enclosed £ .... (cheques should be made payable to 'BRF')

Please charge my MasterCard / Visa ☐ Debit card ☐ with £ ....

Card no. ☐☐☐☐ ☐☐☐☐☐ ☐☐☐☐ ☐☐☐☐

Valid from ☐☐/☐☐ Expires ☐☐/☐☐ Security code* ☐☐☐

Last 3 digits on the reverse of the card

Signature* .... Date ....../....../......

*ESSENTIAL IN ORDER TO PROCESS YOUR PAYMENT

To set up a Direct Debit, please also complete the Direct Debit instruction on page 159 and return it to BRF with this form.

Please return this form with the appropriate payment to:
BRF, 15 The Chambers, Vineyard, Abingdon OX14 3FE

To read our terms and find out about cancelling your order, please visit **brfonline.org.uk/terms**.

The Bible Reading Fellowship is a Registered Charity (233280)

ND0218

NEW DAYLIGHT GIFT SUBSCRIPTION FORM

☐ I would like to give a gift subscription (please provide both names and addresses):

Title .... First name/initials .... Surname ....

Address ....

....

Postcode ....

Telephone .... Email ....

Gift subscription name ....

Gift subscription address ....

.... Postcode ....

Gift message (20 words max. or include your own gift card):

....

....

Please send *New Daylight* beginning with the September 2018 / January 2019 / May 2019 issue (delete as appropriate):

(please tick box)	UK	Europe	Rest of world
New Daylight 1-year subscription	☐ £16.95	☐ £25.20	☐ £29.10
New Daylight 3-year subscription	☐ £46.35	N/A	N/A
New Daylight Deluxe	☐ £21.45	☐ £32.25	☐ £38.25

Total enclosed £ .... (cheques should be made payable to 'BRF')

Please charge my MasterCard / Visa ☐ Debit card ☐ with £ ....

Card no. ☐☐☐☐ ☐☐☐☐ ☐☐☐☐ ☐☐☐☐

Valid from ☐☐☐☐ Expires ☐☐☐☐ Security code* ☐☐☐

Last 3 digits on the reverse of the card

Signature* .... Date ------ / ------ / ------

*ESSENTIAL IN ORDER TO PROCESS YOUR PAYMENT

To set up a Direct Debit, please also complete the Direct Debit instruction on page 159 and return it to BRF with this form.

Please return this form with the appropriate payment to:

BRF

BRF, 15 The Chambers, Vineyard, Abingdon OX14 3FE

To read our terms and find out about cancelling your order, please visit brfonline.org.uk/terms.

The Bible Reading Fellowship is a Registered Charity (233280)

DIRECT DEBIT PAYMENT

You can pay for your annual subscription to our Bible reading notes using Direct Debit. You need only give your bank details once, and the payment is made automatically every year until you cancel it. If you would like to pay by Direct Debit, please use the form opposite, entering your BRF account number under 'Reference number'.

You are fully covered by the Direct Debit Guarantee:

The Direct Debit Guarantee

- This Guarantee is offered by all banks and building societies that accept instructions to pay Direct Debits.

- If there are any changes to the amount, date or frequency of your Direct Debit, The Bible Reading Fellowship will notify you 10 working days in advance of your account being debited or as otherwise agreed. If you request The Bible Reading Fellowship to collect a payment, confirmation of the amount and date will be given to you at the time of the request.

- If an error is made in the payment of your Direct Debit, by The Bible Reading Fellowship or your bank or building society, you are entitled to a full and immediate refund of the amount paid from your bank or building society.

- If you receive a refund you are not entitled to, you must pay it back when The Bible Reading Fellowship asks you to.

- You can cancel a Direct Debit at any time by simply contacting your bank or building society. Written confirmation may be required. Please also notify us.